# BLACK BALLOONS

## *Will Pop for Freedom*

Kristi Cronin

WESTBOW
P R E S S®
A DIVISION OF THOMAS NELSON
& ZONDERVAN

This book is a work of non-fiction. Unless otherwise noted, the author and the publisher make no explicit guarantees as to the accuracy of the information contained in this book and in some cases, names of people and places have been altered to protect their privacy.

WestBow Press books may be ordered through booksellers or by contacting:

WestBow Press
A Division of Thomas Nelson & Zondervan
1663 Liberty Drive
Bloomington, IN 47403
www.westbowpress.com
1 (866) 928-1240

Because of the dynamic nature of the Internet, any web addresses or links contained in this book may have changed since publication and may no longer be valid. The views expressed in this work are solely those of the author and do not necessarily reflect the views of the publisher, and the publisher hereby disclaims any responsibility for them.

Any people depicted in stock imagery provided by Getty Images are models, and such images are being used for illustrative purposes only. Certain stock imagery © Getty Images.

Book Cover Design: Evan Lobalbo
Book Cover Photo: Danette Anderson
Cover Design Concept: Misty McCall
Author Bio Photo: Mike Ramos

Scriptures taken from the Holy Bible, New International Version®, NIV®. Copyright © 1973, 1978, 1984, 2011 by Biblica, Inc.™ Used by permission of Zondervan. All rights reserved worldwide. www.zondervan.com The "NIV" and "New International Version" are trademarks registered in the United States Patent and Trademark Office by Biblica, Inc.™

ISBN: 978-1-9736-7796-3 (sc)
ISBN: 978-1-9736-7797-0 (hc)
ISBN: 978-1-9736-7795-6 (e)

Library of Congress Control Number: 2019917806

Print information available on the last page.

WestBow Press rev. date: 12/19/2019

This book is dedicated to my son, Jude. Because of you, I am free. God lent you to us for a profound purpose, and we cannot wait to see the impact you will have on this world. Know that you are loved beyond measure, not only by your dad and me but also by your Heavenly Father, who created you intricately and perfectly in his image. There is no limit to what you can do. You have been anointed and appointed, my son, and I could not be more thankful that God chose you for our family.

# Contents

# Acknowledgments

Thank you to my incredible husband, my person. Without you, I could never have made it through this project. Thank you for letting me share parts of our lives in hopes of helping and encouraging others. I am in awe of your growth and tenacity this year. I am so grateful to have you as my husband. Thank you for doing life with me and supporting my ideas, no matter how crazy they are.

Thank you to my kiddos, Jude and Camila. You are my life, and I can't believe I get to be your mom. You both have such exciting things ahead of you, and I can't wait to see how God uses you. Thank you for loving and motivating me to be the best version of myself every day. I hope that I can show you that there are no limits to what you can do in this lifetime.

Thank you to my friends, family, and small group that have supported me in this process. You have taken time out of your lives to read this in its raw form, offer feedback and encouragement, and stand by me when I have wanted to give up. You all know who you are and know what a blessing you are to me.

Thank you to my step dad, brother and sister. You are the family God knew I needed and I could not imagine life without you.

Thank you to my *nano*. You are an exemplary husband, father, and grandfather. I don't know how I got so lucky to have had you in my life this long. You have spent one hundred years on this earth, but holy cow, am I grateful. You will never know how much you mean to me and how much I appreciate all that you have done for me.

Thank you to my mom. You are a saint, and the love and compassion you have shown me throughout my life are beyond incredible. I am so lucky to be your daughter and hope that I make you feel proud of me. You have believed in me and supported me from day one. Your love for the Lord and your life keep me inspired. You exemplify all the attributes of an incredible wife and are a true friend to everyone that you encounter. You are the best daughter possible to your dad. You have no idea how much you mean to those around you.

Thank you to my dad for allowing me to share our story so that it will help and impact others. I am grateful to be your daughter. Thank you for sharing so openly with me and walking with me through this writing process. You are a man of integrity, and I love you.

# Introduction

You may ask what qualifies me to write a book. The answer is well nothing really (Insert girl with her hands up in the questioning position emoji here. She's pretty much my favorite one). Honestly though, there is nothing. I'm no one special, I don't have a million followers on Instagram, I'm not the leader of a large church, I don't own my own business, I don't run a nonprofit, and I haven't exactly done things that one would consider out of the ordinary.

I'm a nurse practitioner, so I suppose that I could give you medical advice, but that doesn't justify me writing a book like this. Fortunately, God doesn't call people who are qualified. He qualifies the ones that he calls. I'm not sure where I got that, but I'm stealing it because it's good, and it's true.

Just as I'm not qualified to write this, there are going to be plenty of things in your life that you're not qualified to do, accomplish, or overcome. So that makes us besties already, right? We're not special, or are we?

I think God has greater things in store for us than we could ever imagine, but along the way, we have been handed circumstances that are less than ideal. Here's a shocker: Everyone is handed these inevitably difficult circumstances at some point, regardless of what his or her highlight reel on social media says. I call them *black balloons,* and they create difficulties, trials, and hardships.

Guess what. Black balloons serve a bigger purpose. They aren't put in your life to ruin and defeat you. They aren't meant to be kept hidden and shoved in the closet of your heart and mind with the door locked. Can you believe that these black balloons were handed to you to make you grow and to make you a better and stronger version of yourself—the version that God sees and knows exists when no one else does? They have been handed to you so that you can relate to and reach others in a way that you wouldn't have been able to otherwise.

I think that I just realized what qualified me to write this book. I have a story, and you do too. I've been handed some black balloons throughout my life, but somehow because of God, these black balloons have been used for my good.

God gives us everything we need to pop the balloons and to be set free so that we don't open the closet and get flooded with a thousand black balloons in our faces over and over again. Don't you believe me? Keep reading, and I'll show you. Go on and pop the black balloons you've been holding onto because the freedom that's on the other side, well, let's just say that there's nothing that can compare to it.

# Chapter 1

## The First Black Balloon

You make your entrance into the world the same way we all do—kicking and screaming while being blissfully unaware of what you will face in this world. You've been busy enjoying your warm, cozy home for the last nine months and then *boom!* Your life begins.

Many of us are given healthy and beautiful starts to our lives. For others, just being born is the first black balloon that they are forced to deal with in their lifelong stories. We all have different beginnings, but for some people, those first black balloons come much earlier than they should.

My first one came when I was eight years old. It was the first hard thing that life handed to me. It defined much of my future, my thoughts, and my outlook on life. It took me from an innocent, happy child in a loving family to a broken, hurt, and confused one.

I'll never forget that day. I was sitting on my parents' bed and was looking at their faces. Their faces were drained and distraught. I had never seen them look this way before. It was as if someone had died. Even in my naive eight-year-old brain, I knew this was bad. Something *had* died. It was my parents' marriage. Dying along with it was the joyous life I had known for eight years. Right there at that moment, I knew nothing would be the same again.

My parents were honest with me, which I appreciate. Although while looking back now, I'm not sure that I was ready to handle

1

the honesty of what was going on. They had promised that they would stay together forever and that the three of us would always be together. I had felt so confident in that. I had felt safe.

My parents had been super involved in our church. They hosted Bible studies at our home, and we went on camping trips with other families from our church. It was a beautiful way to do life. But what if all that beauty wasn't real? How do you process the fact that nothing was as you thought it was? How do you come back from that?

Well in my case, it wasn't real. My dad had been having several affairs since the start of my parents' marriage. He was unfaithful. He *was* the man who hosted Bible study but did the opposite of all that was holy. I emphasized the word *was* in that previous sentence because I will write more on that later. It's a big part of the freedom in this story. I think he waited awhile to tell me all of this. I don't remember how old I was when I found out the messy details of my parents' situation.

Now, the eight-year-old me sat on the bed when they first told me they were going to separate, and I was shattered and confused. The day before, we had been a happy family. Minutes before that conversation, we had been a happy family in my mind. I was, handed a black balloon, when up until then, all I had seen were rainbows, puppies, and maybe a few unicorns. My world stopped at that moment. I felt broken and unsure of what would come next.

My parents separated for a while. My mom was broken and sad in a way that a woman and mother should never be. I wanted to fix it for her. I wanted to do something to help her feel better. At that time, I would have done anything to have my life back as it had been before the conversation that had changed everything. I think my mom knew that. She must have because she allowed my dad to move back in and work on restoring something that had been broken beyond recognition.

The year that followed was one of the most difficult ones that I can remember in my childhood. We were together again and living in the same house, but the distance among the three of us was palpable. Nothing was the same.

My mom tried so hard. She wanted to love my father again unconditionally. She wanted to trust him and live just as it had been before the affair explosion. She hid it well. She didn't miss a beat when it came to me. She was always there, cheered me on, listened to me, and supported me. My dad seemed to be trying his hardest too. Still, my parents' connection was gone, and I could tell that it was.

One night, nine-year-old me got tired of seeing my mom being sad, worn out, and drained from trying to rebuild something that had been broken into a million pieces. I told her, "Let's go."

I remember that she looked at me and said, "What?"

I said it again. "Let's go. We should go stay with Nano and Abuela" (my mom's parents who were everything to me). The funny thing was that she didn't fight it. We left that night. I think that it was just what she needed to hear so that she could finally admit that this was no way to live.

The whole year had been painful for all of us. It was full of family counseling. I'm sure my parents went through tons of counseling alone and together. I can only imagine how difficult it was for them to stay afloat during this time—going to work each day, putting on a brave face, and continuing to trudge through life while everything was breaking inside of them.

To be honest, the night we left, I felt relieved. I was happy to be at my grandparents' house. It's interesting that as an eight-year-old, I couldn't completely process what was happening. I knew it was over. From that point on, we would never be a family again. I could never have imagined the effect that this black balloon would have on my life and how I interpreted the world, faith, God, the church, and relationships. This one thing had a ginormous effect on me. The first black balloon would take years for me to process. It would take multiple counselors, psychologists, psychiatrists, and at one point, medication to help me navigate life.

So where does freedom come in, and how did this black balloon finally get popped for good? Keep reading. I promise that I'll give you the good stuff. God gave it to me, and it would be wrong not to share it with you.

## *The Balloon Pops*

What if I told you God used this first difficult black balloon to define my faith? He used it to create freedom in forgiveness, which I could never have found on my own.

I spent years forgiving my dad on the surface. I would act fine toward him. We would laugh and spend time together, and then I would move on, feeling as if this surface-level relationship was all that could ever exist for us. I would tell myself that I had forgiven him, but deep down, I harbored so much anger, frustration, and pain.

These lovely feelings would typically rear their heads at awkward times: when I dated someone or felt friends might be turning their backs on or lying to me. To say that I had some trust issues would be an understatement. The unforgivingness that I had for my father at some point spilled over into just about every relationship that I had. It became evident that I hadn't really forgiven him and still had a lot of work to do.

This feeling of unforgivingness had been affecting my marriage and was still deeply affecting me. I decided that it was time to go back to counseling for the millionth time. This time—really for the first time—I took it seriously. I met with a Christian counselor. I called her the goddess of wisdom. We met every week for three months. I ponied up the dough for it because she didn't accept insurance, and yes, y'all, it was worth every stinking penny. She pushed me to go deep, to do assignments, and to work on myself and my walk with Christ. My walk with Christ was still new. I had only fully surrendered to Christ about three years before this. Don't worry. I'll tell you all about that ultimate freedom in another chapter.

By going through this process and finally surrendering to God's pull, I did it. I forgave my dad fully and completely. I'm talking totally free. I had no more anger and experienced a love-the-man-to-death forgiveness. People ask if that's possible. I get it. I used to wonder that myself. Now I get to live it. The Holy Spirit is real. He moves in you, fills you, and gives you love and joy that cannot be explained.

Together, my dad and I have grown and have let our relationship land in God's hands. We have let God define our relationship and create an undeniable bond after years of disconnect. When we talk, they aren't just surface-level conversations. We pray together and share life.

If you had told eight-year-old me that this was possible, I would never have believed you, but my dad is free. He loves the Lord and is loved back. He doesn't walk in his past. It's there, and we're both reminded of it often, but we're free. The pain is dim, and the connection is strong. The restoration is not something that we could have ever done on our own. That black balloon is popped for good.

That's where the freedom is. God works in every aspect of your life and uses your deepest pain to become your strength. It's God placing key players in your life when you don't even realize it. These anointed people come to revive you.

My goddess of wisdom was that for me. She helped me to see Christ in a way that I hadn't before. She helped me to fully forgive when I didn't think it was possible.

My relationship with my dad is the freedom. My enduring through my parents' divorce and the pain it brought have made me who I am. They made me more durable and able to relate to others who are facing similar challenges. They defined me but also grew me.

Yes, I still have difficult days, and the struggle can be very real, but the freedom that came when I allowed God to come in and to take over this area of my life is better than you could ever imagine. This black balloon haunted me and affected every area of my life well into my thirties. It wasn't easy to overcome. I'll tell you more about my battles as we go.

This first black balloon didn't pop instantly for me. It was more like a pinhole that God made. Over several years, he allowed small amounts of air to seep out, which brought me closer to holding a deflated and overcome black balloon in my hand. Every so often, air has tried to reinflate that first black balloon, but it can't. The balloon has popped and is never coming back.

## *It's Your Turn*

What was the first black balloon in your life?

_____

_____

_____

_____

In what ways did this define you and how you saw the world?

_____

_____

_____

_____

What lies have you told yourself throughout your life because of this first black balloon?

_____

_____

_____

_____

If your first black balloon has a slow leak, what could you specifically ask God to reveal so that you can finally pop it?

_____

_____

_____

_____

How has God used this to grow you?

_____

_____

_____

_____

If you've already popped this balloon, what freedom and good have you found from it?

_____

_____

_____

_____

# Words to Help You Pop the Black Balloon

So do not fear, for I am with you; do not be dismayed, for I am your God. I will strengthen you and help you; I will uphold you with my righteous right hand. (Isaiah 41:10 NIV)

Whoever dwells in the shelter of the Most High will rest in the shadow of the Almighty. (Psalm 91:1 NIV)

It is for freedom that Christ has set us free. Stand firm, then, and do not let yourselves be burdened again by a yoke of slavery. (Galatians 5:1 NIV)

So if the Son sets you free, you will be free indeed. (John 8:36 NIV)

# Chapter 2

# The Black Balloon of Friendship

I've been told that you can count your true friends on one hand. This is probably accurate for most of us. For some, it may be a little more or a little less. If you're running around with twenty solid girlfriends, then girl, I would love to know your secret of how you created and maintained that?

I alluded to my trust issues in the previous chapter, and let me tell you, they run deep. Not only have they affected my romantic relationships but my friendships as well. With growth and maturity, I think I've gotten a little better. We would have to ask one of my close girlfriends to know for sure.

For a long time in my life, I suffered from puppy-cradle-death syndrome (That's not a real thing. I made it up). Puppy-cradle-death syndrome is when you love something so much you smother it—sometimes to death. In this case, the death of a friendship would be the result. If that was a real diagnosis, I had it, and I still do to some degree. I grew up wanting each of my friends to be my best friend.

Did I also mention that I'm an only child? Yeah, I know, that probably explains a lot. You can file a lot of this under reasons why we had two children.

Anyway, I would make a friend and then just about smother that person to death. I wanted to be her number one and never be pushed aside—puppy-cradle-death syndrome. When my friend would try to get some wiggle room, my grip would tighten. I know that this was not very healthy.

Friendships began to carry the heavy weight of importance in my life. Each friend was separate but super important to me. My self-worth was often defined by having friends that needed me or trusted me enough to tell their stuff to. Being left out was my biggest nightmare.

Not everyone will be able to relate to needing to be a number-one friend. Maybe you are more of an introvert and enjoy your space. Maybe you have close friends but are fine with not having them at the forefront of your life. In whatever way you view or do friendship, I think we have at least one thing in common: We've been hurt by someone who was close to us.

This pain seemed magnified to me. This pain cut deep and took a long time for me to comprehend. It has taken some research and soul-searching to discover what God's idea of friendship and community is and how I can apply that to my life. I had to find out how I could walk fully in Christ and get my self-worth from his love and what he said about me as opposed to my girlfriends and those around me? This wasn't easy, my friend. It was doable, but again, I had to go through some things to get there.

The friendship black balloon is the one that comes in, flips you upside down, causes pain, and may even leave you with one less friend. God knows what he is doing. He places people in our lives for a reason. Sometimes he removes them and uses the space that they left behind for a different purpose. You may have more than one friendship black balloon floating around. It's probably about time for you to pop it.

I remember the first time that the concept of having a best friend became real to me. In kindergarten, I became friends with another little girl, and we quickly became inseparable. We did most everything together at school, and our parents started arranging play dates for us. I loved going to her house to play because she had an older brother and sister. I thought it was so cool that there was always commotion and someone around. My parents did a great job of keeping me busy, but it was just them and me in our home. It was fun to be around so many other kids and experience what their family was like.

This great friendship lasted until third grade when her family moved. I remember being sad. I was only about eight years old, but the emotions I experienced as that friend exited my life were very real. Shortly after they moved, my parents' separation began and ultimately their divorce.

It's incredible to look back on events and realize how they affect us. The events of our lives affect how we process the world and others.

My feelings during that time were rooted in loss and change. I couldn't quite express or comprehend what I was feeling, but it wasn't good. I went on to make several other friends using my puppy-cradle-death technique. Throughout my life, I held onto the idea that once I made a close friend, I had to keep them forever, no matter what it took. I didn't want to be left behind or abandoned.

It has been a long process to learn and realize that God creates some friendships to be seasonal. He places key people in our lives at certain times and for certain reasons. For me to learn and understand this, he gave me a friendship black balloon. It was extremely painful. I hated every second of what that friendship's loss entailed, but ultimately, God gave me the tools to pop that black balloon and find what he desired for me to know on the other side of it.

I made friends with this particular girl when we were little— probably around seven years old. We had several things in common, and life with her was super fun. The inside jokes came easily. The world was brighter when we were walking through it together. We went to different schools but still had a close friendship that lasted. We had typical grade-school arguments and issues, but they would pass, and we pressed on. I eventually changed high schools to be at hers.

Let's just say I didn't peak in high school. Those were not my best years. I was fully aware of the tension in our friendship. However, my good old puppy-cradle-death syndrome wouldn't let me branch out. It became increasingly painful to think of how we might not always be friends or be in each other's lives.

When it was time for college, we went together. I don't know if you know this, but college is a crazy time in life. It's a weird time when you're trying to figure major things out while still trying to stay sane.

Again, I struggled. My walk with Christ at that time was not what it is today. I made a lot of ridiculous choices and decisions. Somehow, we stayed friends through this. There were some really ugly moments, but there were also some bright and beautiful times when our friendship just made sense. We endured some major life challenges and disruptions by each other's side.

When you grow up with someone in that way, you're invested. It's not easy to think of life differently or without that person in it. Even if it's unhealthy for both of you, it's familiar. That is not something that anyone turns away from without a fight—and fight we did, via text.

It was the dreaded text match where you send words back and forth, which are then permanently available for you to read over and over. Words are texted that can't be taken back or reworded, no matter how bad you want to. It's important to grasp that no one person is ever at fault in these situations. It always takes two. I am certainly no angel. I have made my fair share of mistakes in friendship and just about every other area of my life.

The friendship black balloon came to me via a text when I was in a very challenging place in my life. I was going through my first pregnancy (which is what ultimately brought me to Christ). I was in graduate school and still navigating a new marriage. I wasn't exactly a friend that anyone deserved during that time.

I was struggling to make it through each day and sometimes through each hour. This took a toll on some of my friendships and an even greater toll on this particular lifelong friendship. I think the rope that was holding our friendship together had been fraying over several years. Each difficult moment and disagreement frayed it more and more. Then during this fragile time in both of our lives, it finally snapped. The black balloon text came stating that we shouldn't be in each other's lives anymore.

I remember reading it and feeling completely broken, misunderstood, devastated, and just plain sad. My whole body was shaking. I felt like someone had died except she hadn't. She was still alive but just didn't want me to be part of her life anymore.

It's so easy in these situations to respond out of pain and anger. The human in me wanted to. I felt like I had so much to say, but because God is good and knows things that I don't, he protected me. He prompted me to put my phone down and to walk away. I walked over and picked up my infant son, whom we had fought so hard to have. I held him while tears streamed down my face.

I asked God why this was happening at this particular time. It felt like too much. My relationship with Christ had only recently, been made real. It was evident that he was there and was working in me. I never responded to that last text. I'm sure that must have been confusing to be on the receiving end of it. I may never know how it was received, but at that time, God guided me to remain silent and let him work.

Sometimes we have to step aside for God to do what only he can do. He's bigger than we are. His plans are bigger, his love is greater, and he knows all the things that we don't know.

This particular black balloon popped quickly. I grieved and mourned the loss of this lifelong friendship, but I trusted God's plan and felt a peace from him that couldn't be explained.

## The Balloon Pops

Losing a friend is painful. Frankly, it sucks for a while, but joy and peace are waiting on the other side. It may take time for these things to come to the surface, but they eventually do. We have to trust God's timing and believe that he is truly good. He is. I promise. It's not that I haven't questioned this because I have. I think it's important that I continue to admit this.

Sometimes in painful moments, it's hard to see his goodness, but every time—and I mean *every single time*—he comes through. I can give you example after example of this in my life. If you take the time to recap and look back over your life's events, you will start to see that there are no coincidences. You will start to see that these black balloons were part of your story and are there to teach and shape you.

My friendship black balloon was no different. After the dust settled, I was able to reflect on my behaviors, on how I handled each situation throughout our friendship, and what I could have done better or differently. I thought about how I would be able to apply this research to other and new friendships. I was able to seek and learn what God said about friendship and community and how we are meant to do it.

Do I still make mistakes in my friendships? Of course I do, all the time. Do I feel left out at times? Yep, thanks to Instagram I do. Do I get hurt by things that are beyond my control? I do, but it's way better than it was. Learning to walk fully in God's grace and comfort and letting him fill me and dictate my self-worth instead of letting others has been the freedom after the pop. It has taken me years. If you can grasp this now, it's going to create real freedom in your life.

God wants us to have great friends and to do life in community with others, but he also wants it to be selfless. If you are experiencing friendship in a self-serving way—getting what you can out of it rather than giving—you're missing the mark. I'm not saying that we should let people walk all over us. I don't believe that is God's desire either. I am saying that we should give selflessly and expect nothing in return. Get your fulfillment from Christ's love and spread it. People are fallible. They will fail your expectations every time, but God never will.

It was several years before I reached out to this particular friend again. I had been reading a book by Bob Goff called *Everybody*

*Always.* If you haven't read it, do yourself a favor and read it. At the end of the book, he challenges his readers to reach out to someone, fully out of love and with no expectations. My friend immediately came to my mind.

I fought it for days and prayed for God to change my mind, but her name came up over and over again. I felt the pull of God on my heart and gave in to Bob's message. Do you remember what I said about key players at key times? God does that.

I sent the message with zero expectations. She responded out of love. No, we're not besties frolicking into the sunset, but I do think we are both more at peace. My love for her never changed. I hope that after my message, she knows that. I think I popped puppy-cradle-death syndrome for good. It might still rear its ugly head now and then, but God has given me the tools to do friendship his way, and you can too.

God wants us to be in community with others, building each other up, providing counsel and wisdom to one another, and showing love and grace to each other even when we don't feel like it. He wants our friendships to be life giving and fulfilling.

He wants us to have a variety of friendships so that we can learn from one another and grow together and on our own. The variety includes having friends in your life that don't share your same beliefs, opinions, or culture. We are encouraged to love everyone—even those that may be difficult to love.

In doing this, we can be fully loved. We can experience friendship and community the way God desires us to. God's love for us encompasses friendship in its purest form. There is nothing better than knowing that you're fully loved and accepted by a Heavenly Father who will never leave or forsake you. That's friendship at its finest.

## It's Your Turn

Do you have a friendship black balloon?

_____

_____

_____

_____

Has God given you what you need to pop it, or are you still waiting?

_____

_____

_____

_____

If you could say something loving to that friend, what would it be?

_____

_____

_____

_____

How do you define friendship? Does your definition line up with God's design for friendship and community? If not, what steps do you need to take to align your beliefs about friendship with God's truth?

_____

_____

_____

_____

# Words to Help You Pop the Black Balloon

My dear brothers and sisters, take note of this: Everyone should be quick to listen, slow to speak and slow to become angry. (James 1:19)

Whoever of you loves life and desires to see many good days, keep your tongue from evil and your lips from telling lies. (Psalm 34: 12–13)

Each one should test their own actions. Then they can take pride in themselves alone, without comparing themselves to someone else. (Galatians 6:4)

Though one may be overpowered, two can defend themselves. A cord of three strands is not quickly broken. (Ecclesiastes 4:12)

# Chapter 3

# The Heartbreak Black Balloon

If dating is your jam and you're awesome at it, I could have used you in my life about twelve years ago. Seriously, where were you when I needed you the most? Dating is definitely not my jam. I'm the worst at it. Still, somehow I landed a husband who continues to surprise me and who endures my level of quirkiness in a way that I never thought was possible.

The road to our love story was bumpy, to say the least. Again, it is important for me to admit this. It would be easy to scroll through my feed and think that we are the epitome of couple goals. Some days we are, but a lot of days, we most definitely are not.

My level of craziness was of a special kind when it came to dating and developing a lasting relationship. After my parent's divorce, I would vow to my mom regularly that I was never getting married. I had no desire to do so. I was sure I would be terrible at it. My fears and brokenness ran way too deep for any dude to comprehend or want to deal with.

Let me give you an example. I went on my first group date when I was in seventh grade. The group was two of my girlfriends, three boys, and me. We went to see the movie *Big Daddy* (It's a great movie, and to be honest, I had already seen it twice before going on this group date).

I had a bit of a crush on one of the boys who was going. He went to a different school, which was great because unlike most of the boys at my school, he hadn't known me since the age of three. He was blissfully unaware of all of the embarrassing things I had done and who I had been in elementary school.

We were sitting next to each other in the dark theater, laughing, and sharing popcorn under the glow of a movie screen. Ah, how romantic, right? Okay, it was cute, and my heart was doing flip-flops. Then it happened—the moment every seventh-grade girl dreams of: He grabbed my hand. I couldn't believe that he liked me. I sat there for five solid minutes wondering if it was even real. It was real and so was the first panic attack I had ever had.

All of a sudden, I felt so sick to my stomach that I couldn't fight it. I jumped out of my seat and sprinted to the back of the theater. Before I could even get out the doors, every single thing I had eaten that day was coming up. It was the king of all vasovagal responses. I was puking in the back of a movie theater because a boy whom I had liked had held my hand. The hand-holding episode felt like an out-of-body experience. I had not known what was happening to me, but I had known that it was an overwhelming feeling. As much as I wanted to fight my response, there was no way I could. It had just happened.

What happened to me medically was this: Some people have something called vasovagal syncope, where they get a little stressed or anxious and pass out. I, however, puke. I know. my glamour is overwhelming.

I stood there for a moment feeling completely stunned and unsure of what to do next. I'm sure that the people who were sitting in the back of the theater heard me, but luckily, no one came to see what was happening. So I did what any self-respecting seventh grader would do: I went to the ticket person and told him that he would never believe this but that someone had puked in the back of theater five (No, I don't really remember the theater number, but you get my drift). I made the yuck/stinky face as I told him so that he wouldn't suspect it had been me.

He did not look thrilled but went and got someone to help him. They cleaned it up. Then I went to the bathroom and tried to freshen up, if that was at all possible. After that, I waltzed back to my seat next to the cute kid that had attempted the romantic seventh-grade holding of my hand and acted as nothing had happened. This time though, I kept my arms and hands off the armrests. I couldn't risk anything like that happening again.

Here's an important takeaway: I couldn't *risk* anything like that happening again. This moment stuck with me like you would not believe. The boy never found out, and by the time the movie was over, the mess in the back was clean, and I had gotten away with it. But like I said, it stuck with me.

I never saw that boy again. It was all just so strange. I couldn't understand how I had ended up tossing my cookies all over the back of the theater when I had felt just fine the entire day leading up to that experience. I wondered if it was just excitement or something I had eaten. As life went on and I got older, I learned what had happened. It had been a case of extreme anxiety. It had been a panic attack, and the only way my body had known how to react to it had been to get sick.

It would be years before this resurfaced because I intentionally decided to avoid the opposite sex for quite some time. Then one particular boy showed up in my life. You know the one. You crush so hard on him that you can't speak when he talks to you and you about pass out when he looks in your direction. I did not want to like him. I fought it but didn't win. He ended up being the one who would deal me the heartbreak black balloon.

I met him when I was fifteen and knew immediately that I had a huge crush on him. He was funny and charismatic. He was not a guy whom I ever thought would be interested in me. A year after I met him, I moved to the school that he was going to. I still had a crush on him. When I would pass him in the hall, I would feel my knees get weak. I don't remember how it happened, but he eventually started to show some interest in me. I'm not going to lie. It was shocking. I had never dated anyone before this, other than during the aforementioned seventh-grade movie fiasco. I hadn't even kissed anyone at this point in my life. Nevertheless, we started hanging out.

One night, he asked me over to his house to watch a movie. Here again was the dreaded movie with a boy I liked. I was extremely nervous. This was foreign territory for me. I had no idea what I should think but did think that he must like me if he had asked me over.

The night was off to a great start, and then there it was: the holding of the hand. I felt fine for a few minutes, and then all of a sudden, I started to feel sweaty and nauseated. It was happening again. I thought, *You have to be kidding me!* I excused myself as quickly as I could and ran to the bathroom. Complete panic took over, and then there I was, having the same reaction I had had back in seventh grade.

I was in shock and completely embarrassed. I couldn't let on that there was anything wrong, or I was sure that we would never hang out again. I thought, *What if he tries to kiss me?* I could have died right there in the bathroom. However, I went back out, we finished the movie, and he didn't kiss me that night. I left feeling defeated and weirded out by my reaction. This was the second time it had happened. Something had to be wrong with me.

It occurred to me that any time I had feelings for someone and they reciprocated them, I got extremely anxious. It took years to work through this and to get to the bottom of it. I was having very real panic attacks.

I thought maybe I shouldn't hang out with him again. I wasn't sure if he would even want to see me again. Well, he did. This ended up being the start of a three-year on-again-off-again relationship. I fell hard, gave my whole heart, and was all in for this kid. During my sixteenth through nineteenth years, my life was consumed with all of our *stuff.* I fell for him against all my better judgment. The anxiety continued throughout our relationship.

I eventually told him about my issues and what I thought might be causing me to react that way. For the most part, he was good about it, but we were both young and lacked maturity. The on-again-off-again relationship continued.

I think that it took over a year before he would even admit to anyone that I was his girlfriend. Ladies, just a word of advice, if he won't call you his girlfriend after an extended period of time and won't admit to other people that he's dating you, you should probably consider letting that ship sail off into the sunset while you stand on the beach holding a glass of wine and waving goodbye.

I continued to accept it though. I stayed on the boat for a while in the hope that he would eventually come out of it and become proud to be my boyfriend. There were times when I think he was, but overall, the relationship was unhealthy for both of us.

I'll never forget that one early evening when I was on my drive home from work. I was going to my parents' house instead of my apartment because it was closer, and I was tired. I had questioned him earlier about something one of my girlfriends had told me, and he had blown it off, which had made me feel like I was crazy. I hadn't thought too much about it but had dropped it.

I called him on my drive home, and he was very short with me when he began the conversation. I could tell something was coming. He broke up with me right then and there. This time, it was for good. I could tell. He wouldn't give me any reason as to why but said that he didn't want to be with me anymore. That was it, we hung up, and the case was closed.

I pulled into my mom's driveway and walked inside. I remember barely being able to stand. I sat on the floor and just bawled my eyes out. My mom came running out of her room and wondered what was going on. I was extremely dramatic; bless my little heart. But it hurt.

That heartbreak black balloon shook me. I had opened up to him and had let him in. Had he had any idea how hard that was for me to do? So there I was in my first relationship watching my biggest fear become a reality. The lies about who I was, who God is, love, and relationships were all there. All these lies flooded my mind. It seemed to me that a committed relationship was a complete joke.

My parents couldn't do it, and now, I couldn't do it either. I resisted dating and giving my heart to someone else because I didn't think I could endure pain like that again. But the pain came, and it cut deep. I was completely heartbroken.

My ex-boyfriend came in and out of my life a couple more times after that. The first love is not an easy one to shake. However, I never gave my heart back to him after that night when I had been so heartbroken. I think I just clung to what was familiar for a little while. I struggled with the pain of whether real love and committed relationships could exist. My parents were the perfect example of a godly marriage until they weren't. How could any relationship work? Why would God allow this to be my first experience with dating? I couldn't make sense of it.

The next few years during my early twenties, I was the furthest from God. It would be wrong for me not to admit that I questioned it all. I questioned his goodness, the reality of Christianity, the church, the people who go to church, whether or not a Heavenly Father could love someone like me, whether all the sins I continued to commit could be forgiven, and if it was really possible to be set free.

It would be a few years before God brought me to my knees and answered these questions. Funny enough, I still went to church most Sundays. I tried different denominations and locations. I was searching. I never questioned if God was real, but I questioned how real he was, and how it was possible to let him take over.

I continued trying to date and still made terrible choices. Even though I was going to church most Sundays, I would roll in disheveled and hung over from the events of the night before. Would you believe me if I told you that even in this, God was pursuing me? Even in the pain and through the wall I had put up to try to keep him out, he was still finding ways to reach me.

He seemed so distant and silent during this time in my life.

Something I have been told and need to make very clear is that even when God seems silent, he's moving. He knows things that we don't know. Even when all seems lost, he uses this pain for our growth and good.

As skeptical as I was during that time, I still wanted to be in church. This want to be at church even when my back was turned to God has been a running theme throughout my life. I still wanted to know more about this Lord and Savior, whom I had been raised to know, but just couldn't understand.

When I started dating the man who is now my husband, I even told him there was no point in us getting serious if he wasn't willing to go to church with me. I met him when I was twenty-one. I remember him saying okay, that he liked me, so he would go to church with me. I'm sure it was confusing to him that I made this a rule in our relationship when nothing about the life I was living looked very Christian. Like I said, it remained important to me, and I knew that if our relationship was going to have a future, I wanted God to be part of it, even if I didn't understand what that looked like at that moment.

The pop was God unexpectedly bringing this man into my life. He liked me and was willing to go to church with me and to try to figure it out as we went. He supported me and seemed truly interested in who I was. Little by little as we got to know each other and sat in church next to each other, the heartbreak black balloon continued to deflate. God saw what was to be our future together when I could not. He placed this key person in my life to ultimately bring healing to me years later and to allow me to experience love and marriage the way God had intended.

## The Balloon Pops

Experiencing heartbreak is terrible. It hurts you to your core and can cause you to question everything. It brings up past feelings and insecurities that you may have tried to bury way down in the depths of your soul. During that time, each moment can seem like days and days can seem like months. You almost have to take it one minute at a time to get through it. Your life without that person is different, and it may not look at all like the life you had planned. The good in it seems nonexistent.

You might be in this place right now. You could be facing a breakup or a divorce and wondering how life will ever pan out from this moment. I get it. It's not easy. This pop took a while for me. It wasn't instant. The healing was a process, but each step of the way, God was there, even when I didn't think he was. He carried me when I couldn't walk. He loved me even though I questioned him. He gave me a person who was willing to sit next to me in church on Sundays even when neither of us knew what that meant.

Over time, my fears about love and marriage became less. This person, who had been placed in my life, became someone I knew that I couldn't live without. I fought it. I broke up with him a thousand times, but he was persistent. I can't help but believe that this was God working in him and us because he knew what he had in store for our futures.

I didn't want to marry anyone. I ran from it, but that changed. After dating my husband for some time, I started to get glimpses of what life together could look like, and it was beautiful. We weren't where I'm at in my walk with Christ now, but we remained open-minded.

I still experienced anxiety and panic attacks. Any time we would get a little closer or emotional intimacy grew stronger in our relationship, I would have one of my anxiety episodes. Luckily, my soon-to-be husband didn't mind my quirks. He took on all the baggage when he chose me, and I took on his. Together we learned how to unpack it with God at the forefront.

Again, this has taken a lot of time, and we still have a lot of growing to do. I still have times where I start to feel like I could slip into a panic, but those times have become less frequent. Believe it or not, I had a panic attack on the night of our wedding. I did great through the whole day and during the ceremony, but as soon as it was over and I realized that we were married and that forever was on the table, pure panic occurred.

It's not easy to overcome our past hurts and what we know of marriage and relationships if our experiences have been less than ideal. God knows that too. He continued to show up for me even though I didn't deserve it. He helped me pop my heartbreak black balloon and give marriage a go. He handpicked my husband for me, which is without a doubt, the obvious truth. God waited on me and continued to pursue me even when my back was turned.

Whatever season you're in right now, let me assure you that God is working for you and not against you. If you're waiting for your person, trust God's timing. Even when it seems hopeless, trust him. His timing is perfect. Someday it will make sense. It's a pattern that he has shown me over and over again. If your heart is broken, lean into him. He will never be closer to you than when you are feeling hurt deeply.

If you've popped your heartbreak black balloon and are in a season of happiness and love, then celebrate because it's awesome and you have so much to be grateful for. There's freedom after this balloon pops. It's waiting for you. God provides what you need when you need it. You just have to lean in and let him do his thing.

## It's Your Turn

Do you have a heartbreak black balloon?

_____

_____

_____

_____

If you do, are there things about this heartbreak that are still affecting you and how you navigate in relationships?

_____

_____

_____

_____

What lies have you told yourself about love and relationships?

_____

_____

_____

_____

What can you ask God specifically to do to set you free?

_____

_____

_____

_____

## Words to Help You Pop the Black Balloon

> But do not forget this one thing, dear friends: With the Lord a day is like a thousand years, and a thousand years are like a day. [9] The Lord is not slow in keeping his promise, as some understand slowness. Instead he is patient with you, not wanting anyone to perish, but everyone to come to repentance. (2 Peter 3:8–9)

In their hearts humans plan their course, but the LORD establishes their steps. (Proverbs 16:9)

Peace I leave with you; my peace I give you. I do not give to you as the world gives. Do not let your hearts be troubled and do not be afraid. (John 14:27)

He heals the brokenhearted and binds up their wounds. (Psalm 147:3)

# Chapter 4

# The Depression Black Balloon

If you're like me, maybe you find it difficult to scroll through your Facebook and Instagram feed and believe that we are a nation that suffers from anxiety and depression. It looks as though everyone is out there living his or her best life and has no time for periods of sadness or feelings of inadequacy.

Those perfectly curated squares and stories paint an unobtainable idea of what life should look like. The vacations, the fashions, the homes, and the lifestyles can be overwhelming. It seems like everyone is doing just fine. We need to remember that these are only glimpses into people's lives. These photos and blurbs don't tell the whole story. I don't know if we are meant to share our whole story all of the time. We aren't given the sacred space that we used to have before technology advanced in the way it did.

I'll be totally honest and say that social media remains to be a struggle for me. It's a love-hate relationship, which I don't completely have a grasp on just yet. I do enjoy it. I love seeing what my friends are doing and connecting with people all over the world, which I would have no way of doing without it. On the other hand, sometimes I scroll through my feed and then leave feeling pretty bad about myself. I start to compare myself with others and wonder why I don't look a certain way or have the level of success that others are experiencing. As I said, I'm conflicted, but we all are on some level.

One thing that is important for us to remember as we scroll, scroll, and scroll some more is that you never know what someone may be facing. That person may be in pain to his or her core while that individual's photos and interactions don't show a hint of it. Even before social media, I fell into this category. If you asked those who went to high school or college with me if they thought I was depressed or anxious, I think that they would tell you that I wasn't. Sure, some select friends and family members were aware of what I was facing, but from the outside looking in, I looked good. I did my best to cover it up.

People can be very good at covering things up. We have a way of showing the outside world that we are doing great while internally, our world is crumbling. I know that not everyone can relate to the experience of anxiety and depression, but I can guarantee that you have walked with someone who was experiencing it. It's everywhere in our culture.

Out of the twenty people who came in each day, I saw at least three or more patients who were depressed or anxious when I was a primary-care provider. Many times, they came in for something else, but the big elephant in the room eventually appeared. Their stories would grip me. I could feel their pain and wanted to do everything in my power to help them. I probably felt this so strongly because I understood what they were describing better than they would ever know.

As a provider, we can empathize but can't draw from our personal experiences, which is important because no one goes to the doctor to hear his or her junk. So I empathized but found myself thinking about these patients once I was home. I hoped that they knew they weren't alone and that sharing what they were experiencing rather than burying it was the best possible thing they could do.

I have the beautiful experience of seeing patients from different backgrounds, religions, social statuses, and sexual orientations. I learn from all of them. Each person's pain and anxiety resonates with me. Each person's life and story touches me.

Depression and anxiety are universal. They don't discriminate. Did you know that Christians experience and battle anxiety and depression? Yep, they sure do. Are you shocked? I hope not because I think this is important to understand. Even with all the faith in the world, this can still be a major battle for a Christian. It's a battle that people fight every single day even after they have accepted Jesus as their Savior. I guess I want you to understand this because I remember being seventeen and in my worst state ever.

I overheard my divorced parents talking. My dad said, "She just needs Jesus. We need to keep praying for her." He didn't say this to be negative or disheartening. He was right. I did need Jesus, but the truth was that while I needed all the prayer I could get, I also needed help. I needed a trusted counselor and community that could support me and allow me to open up. I needed to not be judged for my thoughts and to be able to speak freely about the hurt that I was keeping shoved down inside of me. I needed my dad to love me unconditionally and to show me that with his actions. Not only did I need Jesus and prayer but also many other things to get me to a healthy place so that I could begin to see all the good that God had to offer.

In my most depressed state, I couldn't see God's goodness. I couldn't feel his grace. If he loved me so much, how could he allow me to feel the way I did and continue to struggle the way I was struggling. It took a lot of help. I'll admit that it also took some time on medication to dig me out of that place. Once I was thinking more clearly, I could start to see God working. Even though I felt alone while I was walking through my depression, I wasn't. So many others were facing the same struggles. I just never knew it.

According to the Centers for Disease Control (CDC), in 2016, there were 44,965 deaths from suicide in the United States. It found that 8.1 percent of adults over the age of twenty endorsed feeling depressed at some point during a two-week period.[1]

Anxiety and depression are real, and Christians are not immune. I think that we sometimes feel guilty as Christians if we are dealing with anxiety and depression because we are supposed to be filled with the love of God and therefore, filled with joy and peace. Yes, you will be filled with those things as you walk with Christ, but you can still struggle with negative emotions, fears, worry, and sadness.

I had to fight hard. God still pursued me even when I was so far from him. He will continue to place those key people and opportunities in your life to lead you in the right direction just like he did for me. This can be hard to see when you're depressed and anxious. He's working, and a time will come when it starts to fit together. You will be able to look back and see the moves that he made when you weren't aware of it.

I talked a little bit about my anxiety in the previous chapter. I can laugh about some of it now because I'm much better. The fact that I would puke any time that my heart went pitter-patter for someone is still amusing to me ... and to my family. However, depression is harder to make light of.

My depression black balloon seemed to come at about the age of sixteen. It floated in gradually and became more and more inflated over the next couple of years that followed. This was around the time that I had moved to a new high school. I left the private Christian school that I had been at since I had been three years old. In that environment, I had been so protected and sheltered. I had started to question if there was more and had felt that I would be better off in a less stringent and religious environment.

At that time, Christianity felt forced to me. It felt like something

---

[1] CDC, *Centers for Disease Control and Prevention: Prevalence of Depression Among Adults Aged 20 and Over: United States, 2013-2016*. Accessed October 2019, https://www.cdc.gov/nchs/products/databriefs/db303.htm.

that I was just supposed to do. I had pretty much turned my back on the church at that point, because of what I had experienced with my parents and my family. My dad's family looked like the picture-perfect family from the outside. Everyone knew his family. My grandparents were extremely respected in our church while I was growing up. Here's the caveat: Under the family's churchgoing facade was a Jerry Springer episode just waiting to come out. Let's just say that our family was messy and quite the opposite of the perfect family that others saw on the surface.

When this is your view of religion and Christianity, it's pretty confusing. I think all of this plus the school move that I made, the hormonal mess that I was, and the on-again-off-again boyfriend that was in my life made up the perfect storm to trigger me. I started to relive and process what had happened in my childhood. I felt lonely and misunderstood, even though I was surrounded by friends. I searched for ways to cope with these feelings. It seemed like nothing was helping.

I was always very athletic, so I dove further into sports, trying to keep myself busy. At one point, I was cheering on three teams and running track all during the same time frame. Exercise has always been a major outlet for me, but at this time in my life, it didn't help. I cried most nights and felt a deep pain that I could not shake.

I thought many times about ending my life. I didn't want to feel the way I did anymore. I also didn't want to hurt my mom anymore. I know that seeing me that way was torture for her. Even though I thought about it, I wouldn't let myself do it.

What I did start doing to cope with my situation was a very unhealthy behavior that I was ashamed of for a long time. I started cutting my wrists and forearms. I don't even know how it first started, but I think it was because I had had thoughts of ending my life but couldn't. By inflicting some small physical pain, it distracted me from the emotional turmoil that I was facing. At first, no one knew. I did a good job hiding it. But as I did it more and more frequently, it became a major problem. I had razors hidden everywhere. I had them in my gym bag and in the glove compartment of my car.

I remember the first and only time I was questioned about it. We were at lunch after a sporting event, and one of my good guy friends saw a small cut on my wrist. I usually wore long sleeves so that I could cover my cuts when they were noticeable, but my shirtsleeve slid up a little right in front of him. He asked with a concerned look on his face, "What happened there?" and pointed to the cut.

I made up some excuse about my cat scratching me. I remember that the look on his face remained concerned. He said, "Hmm, ok," and changed the subject. I knew that he didn't believe me and that I had to stop. How had this become part of my life? I knew that I had so much to be grateful for. Why was I so sad and confused?

I finally told my mom what was going on. She was so glad that I did and was very understanding, but I could see that it hurt her to know about it. It was time to go back to counseling. This time, I would see a psychologist and a psychiatrist.

I started on Paxil. I'm not going to lie. This is my least favorite SSRI (selective serotonin reuptake inhibitor) to prescribe as a health care provider because of my own experience with it. Don't get me wrong. It was helpful, but the side effects were awful and coming off it was not an easy task. However, it's important to understand that at that time in my life, it was the right thing to do. It allowed my mind to take a break from my overwhelming thoughts and sadness long enough to start thinking more logically. I was able to start feeling motivated again and to experience gratitude. These were things I hadn't been able to do for quite some time. The depression black balloon was starting to deflate.

I still wasn't sure about my faith during this time of healing, but I knew God was there. I prayed often but struggled to feel his presence. He seemed to be silent, but at times, I could feel his peace. Instead of cutting, I continued to work out and started to talk. I let people know that behind the great grades and accomplishments there was an eight-year-old who was still struggling to process all the things that had happened in her family.

Even though God felt distant from me, he was there. He protected me from really hurting myself. He placed my friend in my life that day to ask me about my arm. He knew before I did that my friend asking me about it was going to set the healing process in motion and keep me from continuing my unhealthy behavior. He began to pop the depression balloon in my life, even though I had turned away from him.

I still struggled with anxiety and depression for a couple of years after that, but it was on a much lighter scale. I stayed on the Paxil through most of college, which I still don't regret. My negative coping mechanisms were in the light now so that my mom could check in on me and keep track of how I was doing. I still didn't go all in on the counseling/psychologist part. I went through the motions, but it wasn't until my aforementioned goddess of wisdom came that I finally did counseling the right way and got what I needed out of it.

Finding a trusted person to share the deep dark things with brings healing. I wish that I would have realized that sooner, but the process of life is done in God's timing and not ours. Fully opening up helps us process and navigate through what we're facing. I never want anyone to feel alone. God will step in. He is there. He will save you over and over again, but sometimes it takes getting help to even be able to see that.

If he can save me and turn me toward himself, he can most definitely do the same for you. Your anxiety and depression balloons can be popped if they are still floating around up there while tethered to your wrist. If you don't have a black balloon of this nature, I'm sure someone around you does. My call to action for you is to be there to listen, to be nonjudgmental, and at times, to say nothing but just show love.

We can live the way we were destined to live and fulfill our full potential completely free from anxiety and depression. It is doable and is God's desire for us. I get to live in complete freedom from depression and to experience happiness and joy every day at this stage in my life. To say that I'm thankful is an understatement. I want everyone to experience this.

## The Balloon Pops

So what sets us free from depression and anxiety, allows us to live in a way that embraces our fullest potential, and helps us keep this black balloon completely deflated for good? Several things work together to allow this to happen. In your journey, God is walking alongside you, guiding you, and lifting you up, even when there seems to be no evidence of it.

He was with me every step, quietly making moves, placing key people in my life, and leading me down the path that ultimately led me to full surrender to him. In my most depressed moments, I couldn't see him. I knew logically that if I prayed he would listen. Then I would feel better, but it was difficult to do. When your view of the church and the people in it doesn't align with what God truly desires for you, it creates a lot of internal turmoil. I wrestled with this for a long time. As I said before, I never questioned if God was real, but I did question his goodness and purpose. I wondered how the terrible things going on in the world made any sense. There are still times that it doesn't add up.

Disgusting things happen much too regularly for us to be able to make sense of them all. Some of you have experienced any plethora of these disgusting things that I am referring to, and like me, you may wonder if you could ever truly be set free. How could a God that loves you allow any of this to happen? Is it possible to live a life without fear, anxiety, depression, hopelessness, and shame?

I know it all seems too good to be true. I felt the same way. The depression black balloon was a big one for me, but I sit here today and write this completely free from it. I haven't experienced a full panic attack in over two years. I haven't been depressed since I weaned myself off my medication at age twenty-one. Life has not gotten easier but has gotten more challenging along the way, but with God's guidance and my learning the best interpersonal ways to cope with life's circumstances, I've been able to thrive, and you can too.

Each of our life's journeys is personal and specific. No one shares the same experiences that you have. I like to think about this because it helps me remember that I am unique and that my Creator chose every step of my life personally. I believe this now because I have been able to watch it play out. I could never have imagined how he could have used a broken marriage, questions about his goodness, and the depression and the anxiety that ensued from it all to set me free, but he has.

As I said earlier, I believe that it was only God's love and his divine intervention that brought my healing. Now they allow me to live in a way that does not include depression or anxiety. But there were other needs that had to be met in order for this pop to happen. I needed to let go of unforgivingness. I needed to find a healthy way to cope with the pain and to let go of my past and my shame. I needed freedom from the unhealthy behavior I had been using to cope. It was important to find a way to share what was going on and to keep from stuffing this black balloon, along with all the others, deep down. All of this took time.

## Ways to Stay Free from This Black Balloon

Here are some things that helped me and continue to help me fight so that I can live completely free from this black balloon.

### 1. Admit There Is an Issue

The first thing is admitting there is an issue. If your level of joy and happiness isn't what it used to be and something just doesn't seem right, try to embrace that. Dig a little deeper to find the cause. There may be one major black balloon or several small ones contributing to the reason why you are feeling the way you do. My realization came from my friend, who finally called me out on my bad behavior by pointing to my wrist, even though he had no idea what he was doing or how that simple moment changed the course of my life.

It's crazy to think and embrace the idea that we may never know how our simplest actions can change the entire course of someone's life. He said something to me. This caused me to stop and truly analyze my behavior for the first time, and because of him, I let my mom in. I stopped this negative coping mechanism, and healing began. It was enough to change my thinking and keep me from causing further harm or ending my life. Once the negative behavior wasn't a secret anymore, I could begin to heal. The biggest thing to remember here is that God placed my friend in that position on that day knowing the chain of events that would transpire.

## 2. Look for the Root Cause

Once you have admitted that there is an issue, look for the root cause. It didn't make sense that events that had occurred when I was eight years old were now affecting me in this way. I didn't completely embrace the counseling I was getting at age seventeen, but the counseling still helped. I do wish the seventeen-year-old me could have realized the beauty in being able to go to someone who would listen and then give unbiased, actionable steps and advice on how to overcome the adversity I was facing. I was too immature to see the importance of this.

If you haven't embraced the idea of counseling, do yourself a favor and try to understand that going to a trusted counselor to help you sort through all of your stuff—and I mean all of it—is so valuable. It's not scary, it's not weird, and it most definitely does not label you as crazy. It's quite the opposite actually. It's healthy and wise and will begin to bring you the healing and freedom that God desires for you.

## 3. Tell a Friend

Consider letting a close and trusted friend or two in on what you are facing. I said a friend or two and not everyone in your social circle. This took time for me to learn. I tended to spill my guts to everyone around me. This is *not* what I am talking about here, friend. When I say one or two people, that's what I mean. You do not need the unsolicited advice of twenty people. You need the valuable advice of two friends who love you, know you well, and will look out for your good. These people should speak truth into your life and tell you the hard things when no one else will but in a way that comes from a place of love. Find these people and keep them close.

## 4. Find Positive Coping Mechanisms

I fill my mind with the following things of God:

- I listen to uplifting podcasts. Not all of them are by Christians, but they do fill my mind with actionable content on how to build a life that exudes potential.
- I read and consume content that builds me up and fills my soul. This involves 100 percent of me reading the Bible daily. It also involves reading good books and dazzling devotions and consuming a social-media feed that fills me up instead of putting knots in my stomach.
- I find time for myself. I know that you are laughing at me right now. I used to laugh at this thought too. I understand why finding time for yourself might seem like a joke when you have a full-time job, a husband, two kids, and responsibilities out the wazoo. That is what my life looks like, but time for me is a priority. I have learned that we do make time for important things. Alone time is toward the top of my list. It may involve getting a babysitter for a couple of hours a week or swapping time with another family to

create this space. Another option is to get up at 6:00 a.m. or—gasp—5:30 a.m. instead of 7:00 a.m. You can look at your schedule and find this little shimmering moment. You may have to make some sacrifices to create it, but it's worth it. If it's important to you, you can make it happen.

- I meditate. Again, you are rolling your eyes at me. Go with it for a moment. This is usually a ten-minute space of time in my day when my mind is free from clutter. It's calming, sweet, and relaxing. They have apps for it. It's far easier to put this in your routine than you think.

- I do something I enjoy. Journaling has been a major source of freedom for me. I started keeping a prayer journal during my pregnancy with my son, and whoa, it is truly incredible to look back and see what God has done. Not everyone enjoys journaling, so this may not be your thing. If you love karaoke or taking a hip-hop dance class now and then, please do it.

- I also have one more very important and healthy coping mechanism: exercise. If you are not moving your body at least three to four times a week, start! Again, I know you are about to punch me through this book, but as I said, if I can make time for it, so can you. The endorphins that are released during exercise create positive feelings and clarity. Exercise helps you release the negative things that exist in you from your day or week. It's healthy.

Here is more about the time thing. As I sit here typing, right now it is 7 a.m. on a Sunday. I have a screaming three-year-old sitting on my lap, but I am going to finish this chapter now. It won't always be easy or pretty, but you can do all of these things if you *choose* to make them priorities. The outcome helps with the pop and the freedom. Positive ways of coping will look different for everyone, but the ones I have shared have been extremely helpful to me. Maybe one or two of these resonate with you. If so, I encourage you to do it and do it now. Don't wait.

## 5. Find a Community

We are not meant to do life alone. For me, this meant finding a small group. Again, I fought this and said that I didn't have time, that I wouldn't fit in, and that it will be weird. Literally, every excuse was on the table for years. I finally put the excuses to bed and did it. I put myself out there. I could not be more thankful that I did. God chose the women in our group. I feel extremely lucky to do life with this group of women who love the Lord and pour into my life as I do my best to reciprocate this to them.

I digress to say that the three-year-old is actually kicking and screaming on the floor right now over egg whites. Most of the time, my life is nuts. I would be lying to you if I painted a beautiful picture of me writing this in peace and sipping my coffee.

The small group has been a huge blessing. I walked into it terrified, but it has been a pleasant surprise over and over again. Surrounding yourself with people who uplift you rather than drain you, speak truth to you instead of gossiping, and listen without judging you is incredibly freeing. Depending on where you are at in your faith, you'll either be open to this idea or not. If you aren't quite ready for a small group, maybe community is a counseling, yoga, or meditation group or a running club. The list goes on. Just join something. Again, I figured this out later rather than sooner. I wish someone had stressed the importance of this to me a long time ago. They probably did. I just didn't listen.

Popping the depression black balloon wasn't easy. You can see how hard I have had to work at keeping it deflated and myself in check daily. Note that this is after I accepted the Lord as my Savior. His love now flows through me like an immense current. As I look back and see how he has worked in my life and how far I am from that eight-year-old girl that I once was, I'm blown away by what he's capable of.

If you're not in this place yet and surrender hasn't happened, I can understand. It's okay to question God's goodness. I just want to encourage you to be open to embracing it when he does show it to you. It may not show up right away, and it may not come in the form you expect, but I can assure you that it will come. If it seems impossible to try to incorporate any of these things that could help you pop your black balloon and live a fuller and freer life, I also get it. I used to feel the same way.

I suggest that you just take one baby step toward doing something that brings you some joy. Start with creating a five-minute space for it. Believe me. We can all find five minutes. Somehow I've been able to arrange a life that allows for full-time work, a husband, a family, exercise, belonging to a community, and things that truly bring me joy regularly. If I can, you can too. If I was slowly able to let God in to do his thing, you can too. The depressed girl who used to cut her arms and hide it and questioned all of God's goodness, the church, her family, and how she could ever be set free is free! The depression black balloon is not a part of my life anymore, and I'm never turning back.

## It's Your Turn

Do you have a depression or anxiety black balloon? If so, do you feel like you have been completely set free from it, or is it still slightly inflated and needing that final pop?

---

---

_____

_____

What positive coping mechanisms do you have? If you don't have any that you currently use, what is one mechanism that you might be able to incorporate into your daily life?

_____

_____

_____

_____

Do you believe God is *for* you and not *against* you? If you don't believe this, I challenge you to write down one way he has shown up within the last week.

_____

_____

_____

_____

Do you know someone who is currently walking through depression or anxiety? If so, what is one thing you could do right now to brighten that person's day? Once you list that thing, go do it.

_____

_____

_____

_____

## Words to Help You Pop the Black Balloon

See, I am doing a new thing! Now it springs up; do you not perceive it? I am making a way in the wilderness and streams in the wasteland. (Isaiah 43:19)

For the Spirit God gave us does not make us timid, but gives us power, love and self-discipline. (2 Timothy 1:7)

Do not be anxious about anything, but in every situation, by prayer and petition, with thanksgiving, present your requests to God. (Philippians 4:6)

For I know the plans I have for you, declares the Lord, plans to prosper you and not to harm you, plans to give you hope and a future. (Jeremiah 29: 11)

# Chapter 5

# The Career Black Balloon

At the end of the school year, my teacher would give each of the kids in the class a character award. You know, it was the everyone-gets-a-trophy award for surviving whichever grade they had completed that year. For whatever reason, this was a huge deal for me. I looked forward to it. I couldn't wait to find out what word the teacher would be awarding me, which described my character for that year.

The excitement would mount, and every stinking year, I would end up with the same word. Do you know what that word was? It was *diligence*. While other kids in my class were getting beautiful words like *kindness, joy, and compassion*, I felt like I was stuck with a boring word, which I didn't understand the meaning of. Seriously, I got the word *diligence* three years in a row. This was between the ages of seven and ten.

I wanted to be this beautiful compassionate soul like some of the other girls in my class and get a word like *kindness*, yet I got *diligent*. Every year, I was disappointed with the word my teacher selected to describe me because it just seemed so boring, but this word was extremely telling of what was to come in my future.

It's quite extraordinary that people can see qualities in us that we can't see in ourselves. While I was doing my best to be kind and compassionate, that wasn't what my teachers saw in me. They saw a tenacious and determined child who couldn't accept no for an answer in just about any aspect of her life. I got great grades, but I worked my tail off for them nonstop. I'm not naturally that smart, but if I set my mind to something, there's no turning back. My teachers picked up on that.

You have amazing qualities that others notice even though you may not. These qualities are what make us unique and help us live in a way that only we can. These are God-given qualities. Even though diligence seemed like the absolute most boring superlative that a seven-to-ten-year-old could receive, it was going to serve me well throughout my life.

What did you want to be when you grew up? Did you want to be a doctor, an actress, a singer, or a CEO? Did you want to do exactly what you are doing now, or did that dream escape you? If you aren't doing what sets your soul on fire, let me be the first to tell you that it's not too late and that you can actually make it happen.

Originally, I wanted to be an Olympic gymnast. I suppose that ship sailed a long time ago. Okay, sorry, that's not a good example of something that it's not too late to achieve. I did go for that goal though. It just wasn't meant to be. Some things just aren't, and it's for our own good.

After my Olympic dreams didn't pan out, I decided on the very practical goal of becoming a nurse. I had come up with this idea for my future while I was still young. Medicine and the human body always fascinated me. I craved to learn more about it. Why didn't I become a doctor? You're not the first and won't be the last to ask me this. At thirteen, I didn't have an answer for that, but deep down, I think it's because I didn't believe that I could do it. I didn't think I was smart enough to become a doctor, and nursing was appealing to me.

Once, I had been in the hospital for constipation, of all things, when I was seven. I remembered the nurses who took care of me but not so much the doctors. I don't know why, but the nurses stood out.

So at thirteen years old, my life's goal was to become a nurse. It seems doable, right? Well it was, and it is, but the journey to get there was no joke. More than once, my career black balloon came in the form of rejection. I'll give you the happy ending before the story, so keep reading.

I'm doing the thing that sets my soul on fire—my soul and no one else's. I'm living out my dream career in real time as I write this. Sorry to spoil that for you, but you need to know that you can have it too. It may not show up in the way you originally planned, but it's never too late. Everyone deserves to live a life that they love.

At age thirteen, I had my first experience with the hospital. My mom worked as an ultrasound technician and somehow found a way for two of my friends and me to volunteer at the hospital she worked at for the summer. We did a lot more goofing off than helping, but the moments that I spent learning stuck with me.

The nurses on the unit we had been assigned to showed us how to take vital signs. They showed us the machine and told us how it worked. They talked about what the numbers meant. They explained why these numbers were important and necessary in being able to know how the patient was doing and if their treatment plan and medications were doing what they were supposed to do.

I ate it up. I also really enjoyed filling the patients' water jugs. I don't know why, but they just seemed so thankful that some kid was doing this for them, and it made my heart just about explode. Like a teenage Grinch, my heart grew three sizes that summer. I discovered that caring for people was a cool thing to do. There the nursing seed was planted. I knew I needed to keep my grades up if this was something I was going to do in my future.

I'm really lucky and have great resources within my family and circle of friends. My uncle was a physician. He would let me shadow him at his practice. My mom would pawn me off on just about anyone at the hospital who would allow me to follow him or her. This included a stint in the operating room, which involved me almost falling on the floor. It was very embarrassing. Y'all, it is weird in there, there are no windows, and I just felt too contained. I think that might have been one of the only times that I have almost passed out. I know that some people love it, but I hated it. At least it was something I could check off my list: operating room nope. Got it. I'm good.

I went to college with the intent of getting a nursing major. I did my best in all my prerequisite classes and made great grades. There was no reason why I shouldn't get into the nursing program. I alluded to the fact that I was a bit tenacious, not to mention a dreamer. So getting into nursing school was one thing, but getting into nursing school in Hawaii and having a full ride to pay for it was another. I decided that I was going to do it. Does that sound crazy? I know. My friends and family thought I was nuts too.

Around this time, I was on the upswing from my depression, so it seemed logical to leave everything I had ever known and move to Hawaii. I was ready for a fresh start, a change of pace, and of course, a nursing degree. I had backup plans. I had applied to several nursing schools, including the program at the university I was currently attending. As I said, there was no reason for me not to get into all of them.

Well, I didn't. I got rejected from the program at my current university. This stung, but it wasn't my heart's desire at that moment, so I was okay with it. It would be too simple if that was the black balloon in this story. It's not. Trust me. It's coming.

I got into two smaller programs in the same city I was living in, which was great, but the big kahuna would be that acceptance from the school in Hawaii. It's the only thing I cared about. I came home to find a thick envelope, which was blue with tropical flowers on it. I couldn't wait to open it. It was the acceptance letter to the Hawaiian nursing program of my dreams. I was thrilled and completely over-the-moon ecstatic, but there was one very big thing I still needed before I could get on that ten-hour flight to my new life. I needed not only to make the cheer team but also to get a full-ride scholarship.

The school also offered 80 percent scholarships, but I had already been told by my parents that it was 100 percent or nothing. We couldn't begin to afford that other 20 percent plus the money for my life out there.

I'll never forget when the phone call came. I was at my stepsister Sissy's high school graduation. I saw the "808" area code on my phone and bolted out of there to answer it. It was the cheerleading coach from the university. Everything stopped, and I hung on every word. I started to analyze his voice but couldn't tell if he sounded happy or if I was about to get the biggest letdown of my life.

It all started blending until I came to as I heard him say, "We would like to offer you a 100 percent scholarship to join our team." I couldn't believe it. Stuff like that did not happen to me. I had many wacky ideas and aspirations, but this was way out of the norm. I waltzed back into the graduation and told my mom, "I'm moving to Hawaii."

Shortly after that phone call, the time came for me to move. My mom and stepdad flew out with me to get me settled in my luxurious Waikiki apartment. Okay, it wasn't luxurious. It was more like a shoebox that smelled like boys, but holy mother of pearl, what a view from my lanai! I couldn't believe I got to live there. I spent the next two days getting settled and acquainted with my new roommates. I'm not even going to lie. It was one of the most exciting times in my life.

The Friday after I moved, I had an appointment with my advisor to start setting up my classes and schedule for the fall semester. My parents were still with me, so they came to the appointment and waited for me outside while I had my advisor meeting. I went into the meeting fully thinking that I would be starting my nursing classes and finishing the second two years of my degree in Hawaii. I planned to cheer for two years and then move back unless I got a job there and decided that I wanted to stay.

What happened in that advisor meeting changed the course of everything, and I mean *everything*. Mind you, I had only been on the island for about four days at that point. We sat down and began to talk about my plans and credits. What came next was the big black balloon that ended up snowballing into a few more along the way in my career path.

The advisor told me that several of my credits hadn't ended up transferring. I would need to retake numerous prerequisite classes before I could begin my nursing classes. I was looking at three to four years before I could get my nursing degree. I couldn't believe it. I had to start all over.

One of my biggest problems was that I knew my body didn't have four years of cheering left in it. I was getting older, and it wasn't as easy as it once had been. I knew there was no way I could maintain a full ride for four years. I had no idea what to do. This was not part of the plan.

I wondered what to tell my mom when I walked out of there: "Hey mom, I just moved across the country on a whim to get a nursing degree, and guess what, my credits didn't transfer, and it's not going to happen for me." Yeah, that sounded good. It was exactly what every parent wants to hear after he or she has spent money on flights, hotels, and moving expenses. I couldn't come up with anything better to say, so it came out much like the above statement. Again, my mom was as understanding as she possibly could have been. Should I have discussed transferring my credits with my advisor before putting all my eggs in the Hawaiian basket? Yes, I probably should have, but it was too late for that, and I needed to figure out what to do.

I was devastated but also realized that this was a once-in-a-lifetime opportunity. There was no way that I was turning around and coming back home. I called my advisor from my previous university. She gave me some good direction.

She advised that I start taking classes toward another degree that I was interested in. Then I could reapply to the nursing programs for the following year if I decided to come back. The other option was to stay and finish out a different degree if it ended up catching my interest. I weighed this option and decided to put my effort toward a degree in psychology. It made sense. I had an interest in it, and it would be applicable if I decided that I still wanted to try for a nursing degree. This situation was far from ideal. I was embarrassed by the fact that I had uprooted my entire life to go to nursing school, only to not do that at all.

Another big reason I had moved was to win the cheerleading nationals. Our team had been number one for the last several years, and it was a known fact that we were a force to be reckoned with. My team got second that year.

Now that seems on point with what God was teaching me, but at the time, I was heartbroken. I was angry and couldn't believe that I had made such a huge move only to fail in the two areas that were my entire purpose for moving there in the first place. However, I had a great year and amazing experiences while living there. This detour ended up being filled with lessons for my life, a lot of surfing, and not much in the realm of academics. Please note that sometimes it's ok to not accomplish much. There is a bigger lesson to be learned when things don't work out. I couldn't see it then, but God did this *for* me and not to break me down.

Nonetheless, the black balloons kept coming. I decided to apply for nursing schools back home after only one year in Hawaii. My body was shutting down, and there was no way I could cheer at that level for another year. I thought that I would surely get into every program that had previously accepted me, even though they weren't as good and weren't my dream programs.

I didn't get in. I got rejected from every single one. Even the nursing schools that had said yes the year before now turned me down. I moved back. I had no place to live, so I was going to have to move back in with my parents. No chance of becoming a nurse was in sight. All the surfing and fun from that year meant nothing. I felt like a complete loser. I had talked such a big game and had followed all of my dreams, only to accomplish nothing other than developing a higher risk of melanoma from all the sun I got that year.

My parents came out to get me and helped me move home. This was so different. There was no promise of an exciting year to come or a celebration of accomplishments. It felt empty. I was terrified to come back home. I had no idea what I was going to do.

I called that same advisor again. At this point, you can see my theme about key people. She was one of them. Her name was Kathy. Bless this woman and the fact that she did not hang up on me. I had been calling her from Hawaii and hadn't even been a student where she had worked. She still had helped me every time.

This time, she told me to finish my psychology degree, and if nursing was still something I wanted to pursue, I could apply to the school's accelerated program after getting my bachelor's degree in another field. She asked if I had enjoyed what I had learned, and I said that I had. The truth was that I had liked it a lot. Psychology made sense to me, and I had had firsthand experience with some of the things I had learned.

Our conversation gave me the guidance that I needed and helped me navigate my next steps. I do not doubt that she was another one of God's angels, which was placed in my life to help me along my way. You have them too. Sometimes you just have to take the time to look back over your life. Then you'll see how God has strategically placed these people in your path. At the time, they seem almost insignificant, but in reality, their roles in your life were pivotal.

I decided to follow her advice and finish my psychology degree. During that time, I also worked as a research assistant for one of my professors, and it was a great experience. I didn't know it then, but this experience would serve me well and be a part of my future.

I started to think that maybe nursing hadn't been what I was meant to do in the first place. For some reason, I felt that God was leading me away from it and that he had a different plan for my life. I still didn't have clarity regarding my relationship with Christ, but I would pray from time to time, and it seemed like he was there guiding me from a distance.

Rejection hurts. It's painful and not easy to get over. I still kind of wished that I could have gone to nursing school, but it didn't seem like it was in the cards for me. I finished my psychology degree and landed a job with a well-known financial company. A good friend got me an interview, and for whatever reason, they were willing to take a chance on this inexperienced twenty-two-year-old bartender with no financial background. I guess the four-year degree that I had was worth something. It led them to consider interviewing me in the first place.

I was excited about the job but soon realized that I hated finance. I had only been working there for about a month and had begun to dread it. Every day, I would walk to my desk, sit there, stare at my computer screen, and think that there had to be more than this in store for me. I should have been happy. Plenty of people would have loved to have that opportunity, but I was miserable. I kept thinking about nursing and helping people. Maybe I was still meant to do it, but how? I had been rejected from every program, but my grades were good. It didn't make sense, but for some reason, it hadn't happened for me. I still wanted it. I still felt deep down that it was what I was meant to be doing. The rejection black balloon hung in the air fully inflated. I didn't know how, but I had to pop it.

## The Balloon Pops

After another month or two of sitting at my desk in the financial company, I was ready to lose it. I even considered going back to bartending full time until I could figure things out. I was still living with my parents because I couldn't afford a place of my own. Let's just say that my entry-level salary wasn't anything to write home about.

Remember how all those teachers were enamored by my *diligence*? They were on to something. One Friday night, I was sitting at home with my mom talking about work and what I was going to do with my life when good old Kathy, the academic advisor, came up in our conversation. She had mentioned that the university had an accelerated nursing program that a student could join once he or she had a bachelor's degree in something else and had all the nursing prerequisites completed. I fell into that category now.

I decided to go online and to see when the next application deadline was. I couldn't make this up if I tried. It was that night at midnight. I looked again and made sure that I had met all the criteria and had all the prerequisites. Sure enough, I did. So I took a gamble. It was 9:00 p.m. I submitted my application by 10:00 p.m., making the deadline with two hours to spare. I prayed because well, I needed something. That was about the only time that I had ever prayed at that stage of my life. I couldn't shake my desire to be a nurse. I had tried so hard and thought I could be happy doing something else, but I wasn't. I also wanted it badly because I had a hard time taking no for an answer. So I submitted that application one last time.

About a week later, I got the e-mail from the school that would decide my fate yet again. This time, it said, "Congratulations," instead of, "We regret to inform you." I got in. After all those years and the rejection, God still chose to answer my prayer and open this door for me. I cried many happy tears that day. I couldn't believe that it was finally going to happen. It wasn't happening in my timing, but it was in God's. The quality of diligence that he had bestowed on me at such a young age was now paying off in a big way. I quit my job at the financial company the following week.

I completed the accelerated nursing program and graduated with a great GPA and a job, which had been lined up in my area of interest: cardiology. I worked at that first job for a year and then felt a stirring in my heart again. I felt that I should apply to graduate school to become a nurse practitioner. Again, there was absolutely no reason why I shouldn't get in. My nursing GPA had been great, and I had recommendation letters from faculty members at the school I was applying to. I also had a great job that was preparing me to take this next step.

I was denied. I was rejected yet again. It felt so unfair. I was watching other girls on my unit get in with no issues while I was tossed aside. I decided to put it on hold and focus on my current job.

Around this time, my husband had proposed. It was an exciting time in our lives. I figured that I was meant to be the best cardiac nurse and wife that I could be. That was just fine. One year later, I felt super restless again. My new husband encouraged me to reapply to a different program. I fought it for a while. I tried to convince myself that I didn't need any more schooling and that I was just fine being a cardiac nurse, but the feeling of being destined for more kept coming up. I finally gave in to my husband's encouragement and applied.

This time, I got in. It happened. Not only did I graduate and pass my boards with flying colors but also was given a job as a graduate assistant during my time in the program. I wouldn't have gotten this role if I hadn't had experience working as a research assistant for my psychology professor. This role allowed me to publish not one but six journal articles during that time. It also allowed me to have one full year of my tuition paid for. I went from being completely rejected over and over again, to a published author. I graduated at the top of my class in our master's program.

I worked for five years as a primary-care provider after graduation and gained experience. These jobs were difficult and served to build stamina and experience in my life. I'm not going to lie. It was super hard at times, but God had something very special in store for me. He honored my diligence and provided the perfect position for me back where it had all started.

I now work as a nurse practitioner in cardiology at the hospital where I first volunteered and learned what vital signs were. My life has come full circle, and to deny God's hand in that would just be nuts. Every step of the way—the rejection letters, a move halfway across the world, and a failed job in finance—he was there paving the path to a place of freedom. Even when I was far from him, only prayed when I needed something, never thanked him, and lived a life that surely didn't show any signs of Christ, he chose to honor me.

If you're in a place where you feel lost and are waiting for God to move and show you what path to take, be encouraged. Even when he is silent, he is moving and working for you. Even if you have no faith and question his goodness, he will still honor you. It may not look the way you think it should, and it may not be in your timing, but it will happen. If you're working at a job that you hate or feels wrong for you, I encourage you to lean into that discomfort. There's a reason for it. It's probably the Holy Spirit stirring you up and preparing you for something bigger.

We all have this insane amount of potential within us. It's there even when we can't see it. I'm proof of that. I don't deserve to be where I'm at, but God had a bigger plan. I still think he does. He's not done with me yet, and he's not done with you. Don't lose heart, stay the course, and embrace that stirring feeling inside you. It's there for a reason, and your career black balloon is going to pop. Freedom is waiting for you. It's in our heavenly Father's hands. He's ready for you to grab it and take off running.

## It's Your Turn

Do you have a career black balloon that you are holding onto? If so, what is it?

_____

_____

_____

_____

Are you currently living out your dream role, or is it still dangling out there waiting for you to step toward it? (Don't forget that this is about you and no one else. Your dream role isn't going to look like anyone else's, and no explanations are necessary here).

_____

_____

_____

_____

If it's still hanging out there waiting for you, what is one small step you could take today toward achieving it?

_____

_____

_____

_____

List one way that God directed you to the path that you are on without you realizing it.

_____

_____

_____

_____

How can you pray specifically for your dream role to align with God's plan for your ultimate purpose?

_____

_____

_____

_____

# Words to Help You Pop the Black Balloon

But those who hope in the LORD will renew their strength. They will soar on wings like eagles; they will run and not grow weary, they will walk and not be faint. (Isaiah 40:31)

But as for you, be strong and do not give up, for your work will be rewarded. (2 Chronicles 15:7)

Each of you should use whatever gift you have received to serve others, as faithful stewards of God's grace in its various forms. (1 Peter 4:10)

Brothers and sisters, I do not consider myself yet to have taken hold of it. But one thing I do: Forgetting what is behind and straining toward what is ahead. (Philippians 3:13)

# Chapter 6

## The Loss Black Balloon

This particular black balloon is one that is still very hard for me to understand. It involves losing someone you love. Sometimes people are taken from us before we're ready. They're taken, and it doesn't make any sense. I struggle to put these pieces together. When I meet my Savior, I can't wait to ask him, "How do we make sense of losing someone we love before it's time?" Even when they have lived a beautiful, long life, the pain of having them with us one day and not the next is all too real.

Two sure facts in life exist. Firstly, each of us is born. We come into the world after our mothers have carried us for nine months. Secondly, we're all going to leave this earth at some point. We don't know when and don't like thinking about it, but it's the hard truth. So how is it even remotely possible to believe that losing someone can work toward our good? Is it possible that when this loss black balloon is popped, it only helps us find freedom and good on the other side?

I know that many of you reading this have lost someone who shouldn't have been taken from you. It wasn't fair and still isn't. There's deep pain there. There's probably also a lack of understanding of how a God who is supposed to be innately good could allow something like this to happen. I get it. I have questioned it myself but have learned some things along the way. God has shown up and helped me grasp small glimpses of his goodness in these scenarios.

I've lost all of my grandparents except one. Losing each one was difficult and had its grieving process attached to it. The last one standing is now one hundred years old. He's a World War II veteran, a husband, a dad, a grandfather, a great-grandfather, a man of integrity, and so much more. He's the man who showed me unconditional love when I needed it the most. I'm close to my grandfather in a truly extraordinary way. He has carried me when I couldn't carry myself, both emotionally and physically, as a baby and a small child. He's been with me every step of the way. The day I lose him is going to be incredibly painful.

I say this because I also believe that the black balloon of loss is relative to the person who is experiencing it. The loss of someone may not seem like the biggest heartache to others who are watching from the outside, but to the person experiencing it, there's a chance it could be the worst pain that he or she has ever come in contact with. We need to be cognizant of this and to allow those around us the space to grieve, no matter what that looks like for them. When the time comes for my grandfather to go, it's going to hurt, but I'll have peace knowing that I've had a discussion with him about the Lord and where his faith lies.

Another important point I want to make is that you may not know where someone is at in his or her faith. My grandfather has a terrible mouth on him, even at one hundred years old. He's rough around the edges, but the truth is that the man is a giant marshmallow. My mom sees him every night in his room praying specifically for each of his children, grandchildren, and great-grandchildren by name.

He had a very bad kidney infection about two years ago, and I knew it was my time to talk with him and see where his faith stood. I went to see him in the hospital by myself and spent about an hour talking with him. I held his hands and asked him if he believed in God. His response was that he did. I asked him if he had ever asked Jesus into his heart, and he said that he had. I prayed with him and then left feeling complete peace and rest in the fact that my rough-around-the-edges grandfather, who means everything to me, would be in heaven. He's still here two years later and going strong.

I may not be able to relate to the loss that you have experienced, but I've seen it play out in some insanely difficult ways among my friends and family members. The points above are important. Remember that in whatever way you choose to grieve and the length of time you need are up to you alone. Don't let anyone dictate that.

Also remember that if you're questioning the faith of the person who has passed, you may be surprised when you enter heaven to find that individual waiting for you. Sometimes it only takes one conversation to change someone's faith. You might have no idea whether that person has accepted Christ or not, but it's very possible that he or she has. It can happen in that person's last moments. Don't forget that Jesus took the thief, who was on the cross next to him, right through the pearly gates, even though his life hadn't reflected love for the Lord until that very moment. That's the grace of God.

Too often, I think that we underestimate the power of our conversations and the impact that we have on people. Your one act of kindness or encouraging words could set you apart and cause someone to contemplate why you act differently.

The loss black balloon is a confusing one, but I still believe that there's a reason and pattern to all God is doing. It's a choice to believe this, but when I've doubted and feared, he has come in given me a little taste of what he is ultimately up to.

One of the hardest losses that I've watched first hand was the loss of one of my best friend's family members. The woman who died had been vibrant, loving, and funny. She brought so much joy with her wherever she went. She was someone you didn't forget easily once you had met her. Her struggle with cancer didn't seem fair. It didn't make sense that such a person would face circumstances that were so far beyond her control. It didn't make sense to see her family struggling during her last weeks on earth.

The pain was palpable and was enough to bring me to my knees in tears for everyone who was involved. I didn't know what her faith was. I wasn't sure if she knew the Lord or what her thoughts on the afterlife were. I had hope that she believed in God and had accepted him but had no way of knowing … that is, until her funeral.

I got there a little late. I was blown away by how packed the place was. There was hardly anywhere to park, and when I walked in to get a seat, I quickly realized that there was standing room only in the back. I found my place and began to take it all in. Everyone in the place was grieving yet also finding a way to celebrate her beautiful life.

The entire situation left me with so many questions. I stood there in awe while trying to take it all in. Each person who spoke about her had such incredible things to say. This didn't surprise me at all.

Her best friend spoke last. She too had beautiful things to say and happy memories to share about her friend. Then she began to talk about her best friend's faith. It was the first time that it had been addressed, and it caught my full attention. She discussed a conversation she had had with her friend about what she had believed. With tears in her eyes, she went on to tell the captivated people in the room that her friend had accepted Jesus before she had passed.

Peace fell over the room. The Holy Spirit was there, and I could feel it. This moment still stands out to me as I write this. It was a glimpse of the good and a small start to the pop of this ginormous loss.

After I got home that night, I spent a lot of time in thought. What each person and family member in that room had experienced during this loss was horrible. Saying that they were heartbroken was an understatement, but I wanted to piece together some good. I began praying for God to show me the good and to help me to try to understand his ways.

Then I had a little revelation. The moment that her friend had mentioned that the woman had accepted Jesus was that small spark. It was a small glimpse of good in this devastating situation. It could have been the first and only moment that some of the people in the room had ever heard about Jesus or had experienced the peace of knowing that their friend or family member was more than okay because she was in heaven.

It may not make sense, but because of her life and death, everyone in that room heard about Jesus. Her life impacted others for good in so many ways. Even after she was gone from this earth, she was a witness for God's goodness without even knowing it. Think about that. We have no idea what kind of impact we're making or can make, but God does. He sees us so differently than others do. He knows the plans he has for us, and even though it doesn't make sense, he's still there working.

## The Balloon Pops

I don't think the loss pop happens instantly. Grieving is a process and is meant to take time. Even years after we have lost someone that we love, we think about and miss him or her. We long for that individual to be with us or to experience things in certain moments by our sides. I don't think that it's something that is supposed to make complete sense. That is hard to admit and accept.

If this is something that you are struggling with, I challenge you to ask God to show you the good. Pray that he will help you glimpse his design or why he would allow such a thing to happen. It's so hard to do because loss is something we have no control over. It's bigger than us. We oftentimes don't get the explanations we're looking for. It takes a tremendous amount of faith to believe that God is for us and exudes goodness.

It took me a long time to get to this point and fully believe that I serve a good God who wants the best for me. Even in my pain, he is working for me. This is true for you too. It's okay if you don't see it that way. He will show you, but you have to take the first steps to let him in.

When I get to heaven and see my friend, it will be an honor to tell her about the impact she has had on my life and on those who were there that day. I truly believe that she may be the reason that someone has faith today.

Popping the loss black balloon comes when we can find peace in the loss of the person we love and can see how that person's life had a positive impact that was bigger than we thought it was. As I have spent time talking with friends and family members about this topic, I have noticed that their stories are similar. They talk about the person's life not being lost in vain but standing for something.

I've heard stories of loss involving drunk driving, overdoses, addictions, cancer, suicides, and the list goes on. While these are difficult topics, the lives of these people were not lost in vain because they brought awareness. Without knowing it, their lives provided education on difficult topics that have saved the lives of others. The freedom from this pop is one that we'll have to work for. It's a process and can be a very difficult one at that.

I think one of the most important things that we can take away from loss is learning how to live eternally. My freedom after the pop lies here. When it's my turn to meet my Maker I hope that he welcomes me in and says, "Well done, good and faithful servant." I may not leave a huge legacy on earth, but what my Heavenly Father thinks of me and says when he meets me matters most.

Losing someone who is close to us is extremely painful, especially when it seems untimely. It may not make sense now or ever in our earthly brains, but we do have the ability to look for the good and to ask God to help us see it. We can ask for his help with the pop, and he'll give it to us. He is a good, good father. Sometimes it helps to remember that his ways are not our ways. He sees things that we don't. His pattern isn't one that we are meant to completely understand.

One thing that I do know is that he'll give you glimpses of the good. He wants you to have faith in him. He slowly reveals more and more of who he is if you will open yourself up to it. His grace and comfort are sufficient for you. My prayer is that you will find a way to embrace this and all the good that he has for you.

*Kristi Cronin*

## It's Your Turn

Do you have a loss black balloon?

_____

_____

_____

_____

What is one way that God has used this loss to positively impact the lives of others? If you can't think of one way, write a request to God to reveal this to you.

_____

_____

_____

_____

What is one change you can make in your life to start living more eternally rather than for earthly recognition?

_____

_____

_____

_____

## Words to Help You Pop the Black Balloon

But he said to me, "My grace is sufficient for you, for my power is made perfect in weakness." Therefore I will boast all the more gladly about my weaknesses, so that Christ's power may rest on me. (2 Corinthians 12:9)

Blessed are you who hunger now, for you will be satisfied. Blessed are you who weep now, for you will laugh. (Luke 6:21)

My comfort in my suffering is this: Your promise preserves my life. (Psalm 119:50)

I remain confident of this: I will see the goodness of the Lord in the land of the living. Wait for the Lord; be strong and take heart and wait for the Lord. (Psalm 27:13–14)

# Chapter 7

# The Marriage Black Balloon

Ah, wedded bliss; it's a dream many of us have, but it's not always a reality. If it's not your reality, let me be the first to tell you that it can be. Whether you are in waiting, seriously dating, engaged, or already married, you can have an incredible partnership that brings joy and is sustainable. You'll likely encounter some black balloons along the way, but a thriving, healthy, and happy relationship is obtainable.

In the previous chapters, I made it clear that marriage was not a top priority for me. The idea of spending my life with one person and it working out was a foreign concept to me. It seemed very risky, and the pain that would come if we didn't ride off into the sunset together would be too much to bear. I used to like the idea of having a boyfriend, but all that forever stuff had me super anxious. I think that I would get myself into relationships that I knew weren't going to progress into marriage.

I had a warped concept of love and didn't have a healthy model of marriage to look to for guidance. Relationships were confusing to me. Even though I had dated some guys for extended periods, those relationships were not headed toward the altar. Having a lasting and happy marriage did not seem likely for me, but God can and will do this even for the most unlikely person.

I continued down the path of relationship self-sabotage until I met my current husband. I was very young when we met. I was just about to turn twenty-two. I know that meeting him was significant to me because I remember exactly what he was wearing that day and the way he smiled at me. I can't tell you those things about anyone else I've met. The funny thing is that for a long time, I tried to make myself believe that meeting him was insignificant. I didn't want to like him and definitely didn't want to fall in love with him.

Well we are nine years into our marriage with two kiddos, and boy am I over the moon in love with this guy. We are in love but not without a significant amount of effort and work. Maintaining a marriage or relationship worth staying in is no easy feat. I want to make that clear because I feel that it isn't always addressed openly. Many times, I look at the lives of others and find it hard to believe that they could be facing any problems at all.

Here's the truth: My husband and I both come from damaged families. We are products of relationships that did not work out well. Our children have seven grandparents (including all the steps). That's a lot of love but also a lot of confusion. We have both brought baggage into our marriage, and to be honest, we've both tried to bury and ignore it. We also didn't let God in to take over until after we had said, "I do." We didn't go to premarital counseling (You gasp. I know that this was not our best move). For a long time, we did things our way and not God's way.

Believe it or not, marriages and relationships can work without God at their centers. Ours was working. However, something will come along that will rock your wedded-bliss boat, and unless you have the Heavenly Father to cling to, you could be going down, my friend.

My husband's and my path to opening up to God and each other is still a work in progress. We get dealt marriage black balloons all over the place. At this point in our lives, we have finally started letting God help us pop the balloons.

No matter what stage you're currently at in life, the one thing that will reshape how you handle the romantic aspect of your life is submitting it to God. I'm talking about full submission, relinquishing control, and letting him get in the driver's seat. It's not easy. It was a major struggle for both my husband and me and still is at times. We both have a lot of growing to do but have also come a long way.

We started out sitting next to each other in church when we were dating. This was something he agreed to do so that he could date me. It was something that I had finally decided was important if any of my relationships were going to work. Neither of us was committed to Christ at that time, but our hearts were open.

Early on in our marriage, we learned that being open to having Christ in our lives wasn't going to be enough to cut it. Surrender is a process. For us, the process slowly started a few months into our marriage when the first marriage black balloon floated on in.

Just after we were married, I began working night shifts as an RN. I was still really new to nursing, so not only was I getting adjusted to being married but also was in the fledgling stages of my career. I liked my job, and I was learning a lot. A great crew worked overnight with me. It was the perfect place for me to start and get some experience.

However, my being gone at night three to four times per week wasn't the best-case scenario for a newlywed couple trying to get a grasp on their new life together. Our sleep schedules were opposite. On my days off, I would push myself to stay awake sometimes for forty-eight hours or more so that we could have time together. To all of you medical professionals out there working nights, bless your hearts and souls because it is not easy! It was hard for us to find a good flow and balance in our new situation.

Have you ever heard anyone say that the first year of marriage is easy and that all you do is fall more and more in love while creating your dream life together? I'm kidding. Maybe some people experience this, but we didn't.

Our first marriage black balloons showed up in the forms of miscommunication, fights over finances, lies we had told ourselves about what marriage was supposed to be like, and both of us carrying a whole lot of baggage, which we should have dropped off before our vows went down. I decided to go to day shift, which was a great decision but still left us a little confused about our flow and time together. I worked weekends, which left space for my husband to do his thing on Fridays and Saturdays. I secretly began to resent this, but wanting to maintain that first-year wedded glow, I never said anything about it.

Then it boiled over, and the black balloon showed up one very early Saturday morning. I had been off work that Friday, so that meant I had to work all weekend. My husband had some friends in town, and they had plans to go out that Friday night. Because we were still new to the marriage thing, we hadn't set up any boundaries concerning how late we would stay out without each other, how much alcohol was okay to have, how much money was okay to spend, and the list goes on.

Looking back, I now see that we should have had these basic conversations before our nuptials. Because neither of us had had a great example of lasting marriage, we had no clue what we were doing or getting into. I think both of us also had the mentality that we could just go with the flow and figure things out as we went. Yes, much of marriage is this way, but I have to tell you that you should probably have some serious conversations about life before entering a lifelong commitment to someone.

So we were going with the flow when on that Friday night my new husband decided to stay out with his friends until 5:30 a.m. He rolled in just as I was getting ready to leave for my shift. I hadn't slept because I had been so worried and had had a million crazy thoughts going through my head. Now I had to make sure that I could keep at least six people alive for twelve hours at my job. I knew that having a conversation at that moment was not a good idea because I was, well, heated.

I left and went to work trying my hardest to keep calm and to push all my feelings aside. I got through the morning and decided to check our newly joined bank account during my lunch break. Let's just say an amount of money was spent the night before that we had never agreed upon. I was already heated, but this quickly turned to fiery and seeing red. Remember that I said our black balloons were a lack of communication, financial disagreements, and a ton of baggage. Well those balloons were fully inflated, and I still had six hours of being a nurse to get through.

I finished my shift and made it home. We had our biggest and nastiest fight to date. I think that at one point, I chucked a textbook at him. Okay, I don't think I did it, I actually did it. We were the worst versions of ourselves in those moments. We didn't have the tools or maturity to handle the situation appropriately.

I ran out because my first instinct was to escape and to try to avoid conflict. This was not a good move. I went to my mom's and stayed there for a couple of days. I remember crying on her couch and telling her, "Well it happened. It's only been a few months, and not only am I as bad at marriage as I thought I was going to be but I don't think either of us can do this."

I started to fill my head with all the lies that I had told myself growing up: I wasn't good enough, no man could ever truly be faithful to me, if God was really good, he would have spared me from getting married only to end up heartbroken, and the entire idea of marriage was stupid. I wallowed in all of my lies and nonsense for a couple of days.

Finally, my husband and I started talking again. It was evident that we missed each other, and the thought of us not being together had us both scared. I swallowed my pride and went home. I didn't pray on my way home. In fact, I don't think I prayed at all during those few days. I felt so distant from God and was full of anger and frustration, but as he does, God showed up in our first conversation when I got home.

We were both calm yet still emotional. We both apologized and then talked about what our next steps should be. We needed some guidance. No offense to our families, but they weren't exactly the best places for us to start. I think that I said something along the lines of, "Do you think maybe we should get some counseling?" This makes me laugh now because the answer to this is, of course, that you should. My husband agreed to it. I knew then that he did care. Not every guy will agree to this. If you are in a situation where your partner doesn't agree to go to counseling with you or on his or her own, please know that you are not alone. The biggest and greatest thing you can do in that situation is to invest in yourself and your growth. Get on your knees and submit the situation to Christ. Do your best to rely on the Lord to work in your partner. As hard as it is to do, trust God's timing. He will show up for you just as he did for us that night.

After we agreed to go to counseling, we started looking for someone to meet with. I suggested a Christian counselor because even though I was somewhat hardened, I knew that we needed God to intervene. Again, my husband agreed, and we ended up scheduling our first appointment at a local Christian counseling center. Take a guess at whom our counselor was. It was my goddess of wisdom. The first time I met her was in a couple's session with my husband. I had no idea what she would mean to me or do for me in that initial encounter, but God did.

The best things she told us at the end of our first session were that we weren't too far gone, that our marriage was salvageable, and that we were going to be okay. She told us that she could see and feel the love we had for each other. We needed to hear that. We needed to hear that we weren't alone and that other couples wanted to throw textbooks at each other during their first year of wedded bliss too. She acknowledged our hurts. She agreed that the things we had both brought into our marriage had not been small. With her help, we started unpacking our junk. We learned more about each other. We also learned how to make our relationship successful and enjoyable.

We started taking church and having Christ in our marriage a little more seriously. I say a little because that's the truth. Full surrender hadn't come yet. God used something that was much bigger than both of us to make that happen, but he was planting a seed. He started softening our hearts and equipping us for our biggest challenge and triumph yet, which came in our son. Our openness was turning into belief. For the first time in all of my years of being a Christian, I finally started to develop my walk with God. I could see him working in our marriage and our relationship day by day. The first marriage black balloon was starting to deflate.

## The Balloon Pops

I believe that we met with my goddess of wisdom for a few months. It was extremely helpful and something we definitely should have done before we got married, but I believe that it all happened in God's timing. We hit a place of desperation after those first few months of marriage. God used this for us and not against us. During that time, we became more consistent about going to church. We had more discussions on how we could incorporate faith into our lives, but we still weren't there yet.

I wasn't seeking God on my own and still hadn't let him take over, but the process was in motion. We had no idea how much we were going to need God at the center of our marriage, but boy did he help us learn that without him, our marriage would just continue *working*.

Everyone brings things from the past into their current relationships. We're shaped by what we've experienced. Often, I don't think we even realize how affected we are and how this impacts the way we handle things in our relationships and lives. Learning about how your partner communicates, what he or she values in a relationship, what he or she has been through, and what makes him or her feel loved and accepted are pivotal things to know.

We didn't understand all of this. We just thought that since we had a great time dating, our marriage would be the same way. It wasn't. There were so many added elements to navigate through, and there still are. It has taken years for us to learn this: to explore how we can truly put each other first and experience an exceptional marriage.

Since I'm being completely transparent, this year has been one of our most challenging years, but holy cow, God is working. He is using our pain to grow us. He has used what could have broken us to build us up. Being able to see and experience this first hand has given both of us an undeniable view of who God is. He really is good. In your deepest pain, questions, judgment, and misconceptions, he is still good. We have a long way to go, but I think we have both finally embraced the process.

So how do we keep our marriage black balloons deflated and work toward popping all of the new ones, which regularly float on in? How do we ditch mediocre for exceptional? First of all, we are both committed to making our marriage the best it can be every single day. We are committed to doing all that we can to avoid leaving a legacy of divorce to our children.

This has not been easy. It takes work and commitment every single day. We both have sought counseling and have met with our pastor and others who are wiser and can speak life into us. We are committed to changing our bad behaviors and working toward replacing them with healthy and positive ones. We've decided that life is happening for us and not to us. We date each other as much as possible. We travel together, with or without our kids. We invest in our time together regularly, and it's usually doing things that are specific to us. Other people may not find the things we do enjoyable, but we do. Having fun together and remembering why you started dating in the first place are extremely healthy and refreshing. It's about the two of you and no one else.

We remind ourselves of why we like each other as much as we can. We work on giving each other grace. We embrace each other's flaws and celebrate each other's triumphs. We set common goals and commit to conquering them together. We give each other space to be alone or with friends away from each other. We have sex a lot (Ha ha! Yeah, I said it. Sorry mom and dad). We talk about what our dream life together looks like and put steps into action to make it happen.

Most importantly, we let God in to take over. We are so far

from perfect, and both of us mess up on a regular basis, but in our mess and weakness, God continues to show up for us and guide us. Crazy hard things still happen to us all the time, but we are much more equipped to tackle them because of what God has done in us. We're a work in progress. There is absolutely no other human on this planet that I would rather be doing this crazy, beautiful life with than my husband. God sees what we can't see. I know that he picked my husband and me specifically for each other to carry out his design and purpose.

I hope that you are experiencing a relationship or marriage that is full of all that God has to offer. I hope that no matter what black balloons float in, you and your partner can pop them with ease and as a team. I hope that if you're single, you embrace it, live it up, lean into God with all of your heart and soul, and know that he can fill and satisfy you completely. No one else can. When his timing is perfect, he will send you your person.

I wasn't the marrying type, and we certainly didn't come from a chain of successful marriages, so if I can be in a place where my marriage is strong, healthy, and happy, so can you. Trust that God has so much more for you than you could imagine. His word is filled with his promises to prosper us. We just need to lean in and let him do his thing.

## It's Your Turn

Do you have a marriage or relationship black balloon that you are currently facing? If so, how can you pray for God's hand in this situation?

_____

_____

_____

_____

If you could have your dream marriage or relationship, what would it look like? What would you do together, where would you live, and what things would you accomplish together?

_____

_____

_____

_____

Do you walk with the fullness of God and all he has to offer you? What is one way you can seek Christ today personally? Do it and then share what you did with your partner or a friend.

_____

_____

_____

_____

## Words to Help You Pop the Black Balloon

There is no fear in love. But perfect love drives out fear, because fear has to do with punishment. The one who fears is not made perfect in love. We love because he first loved us. (1 John 4:18–19)

Be completely humble and gentle; be patient, bearing with one another in love. (Ephesians 4:2)

A foolish child is a father's ruin, and a quarrelsome wife is like the constant dripping of a leaky roof. (Proverbs 19:13)

Taste and see that the Lord is good; blessed is the one who takes refuge in him. (Psalm 34:8)

# Chapter 8

# The Surrender Black Balloon

Faith and the church have been things that I have questioned since I was very young. After being handed my first black balloon, my faith was not only shaken but was diminished. At times, it was nonexistent. I believed in God, but I spent many years picking and choosing when I would let him in or if I wanted to be a Christian that day. I had such a warped view of Christianity and the church. Try as I may, I couldn't seem to find my place. I made bad decision after bad decision, yet my Savior pursued me.

So many times, I would finally start to believe and to give him an inch, and even though I didn't deserve it, he would take that inch and bless me immensely. The pattern of God's presence in my life has been undeniable. When you take the time to reflect and to see what you've been saved from and what difficult circumstances you have faced only to come out in a place that screams redemption, there's no denying God's existence or hand in it all.

I'm an unlikely believer who has been hurt and has seen the disgraceful inner workings of a Christian family and the church. I have witnessed hypocrisy at its finest and seen how someone can proclaim the gospel but live the opposite. Yet I still couldn't write my faith off completely.

In Matthew 17:20, Jesus talks about having faith the size of a mustard seed and that that is enough to move mountains and do anything. I carried a small mustard seed of faith for years. There were so many times that I wanted to let go of my faith and do everything on my own, but for some reason, I still found myself in church on Sundays.

Many times, I was more of an observer. I watched the pastor to see how he taught or acted. I would watch his wife and family and wonder if he was truly who he said he was. I would look around at the congregation and wonder who was there for God and who was there to check a box. I would church hop and eventually decide that each one wasn't for me. Plenty of Sundays, I'd show up hungover and probably wreaking of the madness from the night before, but for some reason, I still went. I'd listen to the messages but never really drink in what God was saying to me. I would find myself returning week after week. I would stop going for a few years and then go back for one reason or another. This went on and on.

It makes sense to me now. I couldn't deny God completely because he wasn't done with me, and he's still not. All those sermons didn't fall on deaf ears. They added up, and I eventually needed to put into practice everything they said. All along, God had been preparing me for this moment in my life, which would be the turning point for my surrender. He wanted to make sure that I would decide to honor him. He had been letting me find my way to him all along. My mustard seed of faith was about to move a mountain. I just didn't know it yet.

My husband and I had gotten to a point where we had been attending the same church each week consistently for over a year. We had been through counseling and were definitely in a much better place in our marriage, but God was still not at the center of it. My faith was mediocre at best, but it was there.

Things were good, and we began to toss around the idea of trying for a baby. I was smack dab in the middle of graduate school. We had about a million and one things going on, but for some reason, we kept having the baby discussion. Mind you, not only was I not the marrying type, but I surely was not the mothering type. I deeply feared bringing humans into this world. I figured that all I would do is ruin them and set them up for a life of pain. But God had a very different plan. I do not doubt that he was the one who was laying this crazy desire to procreate heavily on my heart.

We decided to stop taking precautions and preventative measures to see if we would soon be parents. It didn't happen immediately, but it did end up happening. Finding out I was pregnant was probably one of the most exciting things I've ever experienced. It was crazy to look at the five tests that I had taken and to see them all read positive. Yeah, I said five. It's because I'm crazy and needed major validation that this was happening. I couldn't wait for our first doctor's appointment.

I decided to stay at my current ob-gyn's practice because I had been going there for a few years. I made this decision out of convenience. A word to those who are expecting a child or to anyone looking for a provider in general, choosing one out of convenience may not be the best choice (just saying). Anyway, we went to our first appointment and got to experience all the magic of it. We heard the heartbeat and saw what looked like a Gummy Bear floating around in my uterus. We were thrilled.

Several weeks passed, and we went for our twelve-week ultrasound. Everything looked great, and again we were over the moon. We left the office and went to get pizza right after the appointment. We walked into the restaurant and the song "Hey Jude" by the Beatles was playing as we walked in. Jude was the name we had already picked if we were having a boy. I looked at my husband, grabbed my belly, and said, "It's a boy for sure. We're getting our Jude."

The next few weeks were great. We went to Hawaii for our "babymoon," and I was finally able to show my husband wonderful things about the islands and the reason that Hawaii held such a special place in my heart. We were so happy. School and work were going well, our marriage was on track, and we were about to have our first baby, who was in fact, a boy.

I couldn't deny that God was in this. I could feel him tugging on my heart. We remained consistent at church, and for the first time in a long time, I started journaling again and praying. I actively prayed over my son by name. I leaned into God a little more. I knew that if he was lending me this child and had chosen me to become a mom, he must love me. I don't know why this is what struck me when he had done so many other things for me and had delivered me from so much, but it was. I began to give more of my life to him, not knowing what he was preparing me for.

We went for our twenty-week ultrasound shortly after we got back from Hawaii. We fully expected this to go just as the others had. We walked into the office beaming with excitement. The twenty-week ultrasound is super important because it is the anatomy scan of the baby. This ultrasound looks for indicators of abnormalities and signs of chromosomal variances. I didn't give much thought to the tests for chromosomal abnormalities because in my head, we were low risk and knew we would keep our son regardless. It's just how we felt. The ultrasound looks for those things whether you want it or not.

The ultrasound technologist was wonderful. I know that she didn't want to scare us, so she stayed very calm. I knew that something was off because she told us to stay in the waiting room afterward and that the doctor would need to see us again before we left. I was extremely nervous during that fifteen-minute wait. It felt like days.

They finally brought us back. The doctor told us that there were several markers on the ultrasound indicating that our son was at high risk for a genetic anomaly. He would be referring us to a perinatologist for further testing and evaluation. The discussion ended with that. The word *ventriculomegaly* was used. I knew enough at that stage in my career and training to know that it meant that the ventricles in our son's brain were enlarged. This was the main thing that I remembered him saying. It was all such a blur.

I lucked out because my mom happened to know our ultrasound

technician. Again, God uses key people in our lives even when we can't see it. The technician told my mom that the other markers were in his heart and his kidneys and that it looked like I had too much amniotic fluid. All of these can be subtle indicators of a genetic abnormality. She assured my mom that they were just being cautious and that she felt everything was going to be okay, but I had a very hard time accepting this.

It was three weeks until we could get in to see the perinatologist. During those three weeks, I researched every journal article I could on genetic markers and ventriculomegaly. I had access to all the databases thanks to my master's program and working as a graduate assistant for the director of our program. Again, this hadn't happened by mistake. God put me in that position to prepare me mentally and give me extended knowledge of what was happening with our son.

The day of the appointment came, and I was a wreck. It fell on 9/11, which was already a very difficult day for everyone. It was especially difficult for our family because we had lost our uncle due to lung complications related to that day and him being a 9/11 firefighter. Even worse, my husband was out of town for work. Luckily, my mom offered to come to the appointment with me. I had no idea that God had been preparing me for what I was about to experience. The surrender black balloon was about to be fully inflated by a hardened perinatologist with an exceptionally poor bedside manner.

Before meeting with the doctor, I had a very detailed ultrasound of my baby boy. Another thing that was not a coincidence in this scenario was that my mom had been an ultrasound technician for about twenty years, so she knew all too well, what she was looking at on the screen in front of us.

Not much was said during the scan, but I remember being able to see my baby's face in 4-D. My heart pounded with excitement, and my nerves settled. It was my son, and I was looking at his beautiful face. I felt like this was a gift. I was grateful to be able to see him, even under these circumstances.

The doctor didn't look at the ultrasound in real time. He came in to talk to me after he had reviewed the images on his own. I felt positive when he walked in. I had been uplifted by the loving feelings that I had experienced while seeing my son's beautiful face. He started out by asking me a myriad of questions regarding exposures, infections, what I did for a living, family history, travel, and the list went on and on. I could tell that the doctor spoke in a straightforward manner—none of what he had to say would be sugarcoated.

He told me that he saw multiple markers for Down syndrome on my ultrasound and that even if my son didn't have it, he would likely experience a severe developmental delay due to the size of the ventricles in his brain. The black balloon was beginning to inflate, but it got worse.

He then told me that since I would be at twenty-four weeks in the pregnancy in just three days, we would *need* to do an amniocentesis as soon as possible. He went on to tell me that we needed to complete the amniocentesis immediately because after that I would no longer be able to legally terminate my pregnancy in our state. He said that if I needed more than twenty-four hours to make this decision, he would be able to help arrange for me to fly to another state to terminate the pregnancy if needed.

The conversation and his approach didn't feel real. To this day, my mom still says that she would have never believed me if she hadn't been there to witness it. I told him that I saw no point in having an amniocentesis because I had already decided that I was having my son regardless of any diagnosis. I knew that I would love him no matter what, so invasive testing didn't seem necessary to me since I was that far along in my pregnancy.

The doctor was not a fan of how I responded and began to get visibly irritated with me. As a provider myself, I do understand that he had to have this discussion with me. I understand that he had to be realistic with me and to lay out all of my options. However, his delivery and lack of understanding of my choices were not right. No matter what patients are facing, it's their body and ultimately, their decision how they should proceed with their care. In my case, we were also discussing my son's life.

I somehow found enough strength to walk out of the office. I couldn't even acknowledge the front-office staff as I walked by. One of the women leaned over the desk and said, "We need to schedule your follow-up," as I was heading for the door. My mom responded for me, thank God, because I just couldn't. She told her we wouldn't be back.

As tears streamed down my face, I stumbled over to the McDonalds parking lot next to the office and fell to the ground. I was five months pregnant, weeping in a McDonald's parking lot, and unable to find any words to speak. How was I going to explain this to my husband? He hadn't even been there to hear anything the doctor had said about what we were facing.

I cried in the parking lot for a hot minute. I couldn't quite process all that had just happened, but I knew that I needed to peel myself off the concrete. I made it into McDonalds and ordered a strawberry milkshake. As I sat there next to my mom sipping my milkshake, I felt completely lost. I had made a concrete decision. I had decided that I would honor the fact that God chose to give me this child when he didn't have to. I would bring him into the world no matter what. But I have to tell you, the unknown was a terrifying place.

Later that night when I could finally form sentences and knew that my husband was out of his work meetings, I called to tell him about the appointment. He was supportive and sided with me in having this baby no matter what. He supported my decision to forgo invasive testing at this stage of the pregnancy and assured me that we were in this together. We also decided that we would get a second opinion. More than ever, I knew that I was meant to spend forever with this man. He understood me, supported me, and shared the same love that I had for our unborn son.

The next day, I was still an emotional mess and didn't know how to begin to continue with life and my obligations. I was sent home from work because I was so off kilter, and let's face it, you shouldn't be in charge of other people's lives when you aren't able to function. I went home and tried to rest. I tried to clear my head and find some sense of peace, but it wouldn't come.

Because I had no other options, I began to pray. I began to use my little mustard seed of faith and to lean into the Lord. Up to this moment, he had been changing my heart. Now I needed him more than ever. I asked for guidance, help, rest, and peace. I asked God to save our son and allow him to be born healthy and whole, if it was possible.

I began to feel a little better, and a thought came into my head. I reached out to my divorced parents and mother in law and asked if they would be willing to come to church with us that Sunday. It was time for us to go to the altar as a family and pray over this little life, which was inside me.

## The Balloon Pops

Everyone agreed to attend service with my husband and me that Sunday. We all awkwardly met in the lobby and found seats together. I can't tell you what the message was about that day, but I can tell you that God was in that place. I had peace that I hadn't experienced in weeks. I knew something big was about to happen.

My appointment with our new perinatologist was that week, and I had been mentally preparing for how this was going to go. I think I even cried on the phone when I had called for the appointment because I had been told that this doctor was the best of the best and that he would acknowledge my desires for our son. I'm sure the woman who took my call for the appointment thought I was nuts, but she didn't sound like it. She was so understanding and comforting. This experience was already different from the one we had just had. My mustard seed had continued to grow, and unbeknownst to me as I sat there during that service, it was about to explode.

The service ended, and I told my parents that I wanted to be prayed over and that I expected each of them to come to the altar with us. Everyone agreed. Although broken and dysfunctional, all of us were gathered at the altar because of our unborn son. The dysfunction faded for a moment, and we were all there as one family.

A man and a woman came over to us and asked how they could pray for us. With tears streaming down my face, I told them the whole story. The woman took out a list of healing scriptures and spoke them over me.

After this, she and the man prayed over us. He knelt on the ground and laid hands on my belly. Even as I write this, the tears begin to flow just as they did that day. He held my belly and prayed the prayer that changed the course of my entire life. He prayed for healing, the release of anxiety, freedom from the pull of the enemy, my son's future, our marriage, our parents, and a peace to consume me beyond anything I could imagine.

His words were anointed, and the Holy Spirit came alive in me in a way that I had never experienced. It was an unexplainable feeling, but I just knew that after this prayer, nothing would ever be the same again, and it wasn't. I was at peace, had faith, and experienced emotional freedom and healing with both of my divorced parents, in-laws, and my husband by my side. It was the most powerful moment of my life.

From that point on, I was aware that I was fully loved and accepted by my Heavenly Father and so was my son and my entire family. The Lord accepts us if we are willing to let him in. Everything about that moment was real. All of us felt it.

The woman looked at me after the man had prayed and said, "Your son is healthy. God is going to honor you." I'll never forget those words. God was going to honor me? After all of my nonsense and mistakes, this truth was hard for me to believe. She gave me the paper that had all of the verses on it.

For the first time in my life, I left the church knowing that I was redeemed and was fully aware of whom God was. I continued to read those scriptures over my son every day. I anointed my belly and prayed over our son. I envisioned him as being healthy and active in all stages of his life. I continued to keep a prayer journal and made a commitment to complete one devotion every day. I felt and was different. I could feel God's presence in a way that I never had before.

The day of our second-opinion appointment came. Even though I was nervous, I had so much faith in what God was doing. I had accepted that it was possible that our son would be healthy, but I also accepted that God may not choose to allow this. I was okay with it. For the first time in my life, I truly trusted him.

The staff members at the office were so nice. The doctor came in with a fellow who was in training and conducted our ultrasound with the technologist. He watched the entire thing and explained everything as the technician performed the ultrasound. He explained that while he did see ventriculomegaly, he felt it was minimal. He did not feel the other markers were anything to be concerned with. His exact words were, "This is a healthy baby. I want you to be able to relax and enjoy the rest of your pregnancy."

He explained that he would be ordering an MRI of our son's brain that week, just to make sure there was nothing else to be concerned about and so that we could have the appropriate measures in place once he was born if needed. I agreed as this was a noninvasive procedure and would only provide more information to help our son once he was born.

We left feeling completely reassured and amazed. We had gone from being told that we could be flown to another state to terminate the pregnancy to being told that our baby was healthy. It was surreal. The only way I could make sense of it was to realize that something had changed during that prayer. It had to have. This was not only a second opinion, but it was the polar opposite of the other opinion. I felt like I was floating as I walked out of that office. I didn't think anything could bring me down. I had never felt closer to the Lord than I did at that time.

So what could possibly happen to change that day? Once you commit your life to Christ completely, things are supposed to go smoothly, right? I mean, I had finally fully surrendered. Life is funny that way. It's unpredictable. Just as you feel you have everything figured out and it's smooth sailing, it's not.

On my drive home, I was giddy. I called all the grandparents and could not wait to tell them the incredible news about their grandson. The last person I called was my dad. As my faith had grown, my bond and my relationship with my dad was in the best place it had ever been. As I started telling him about the appointment and the miracles God was giving us. Suddenly, a car was coming at me in the opposite direction. I know that this sounds made up, but I assure you that it's not. This is real-life stuff, which goes on and can happen at any moment.

I dropped my phone and swerved my little green Volkswagen bug straight into a wall on the interstate. I had missed the car that had been coming at me. Somehow by God's grace, the airbag hadn't deployed. I had hit the upper right side of my ribs on the steering wheel, completely missing my large pregnant belly.

I sat there stunned. I couldn't believe what had just happened. I immediately began crying out to God and begging him to allow me to feel my son kick. I sat there completely still while I waited to feel those kicks, which at times, I had previously found annoying. How stupid I had been. How could I have thought that it was annoying to feel my son moving? I was desperate in those brief moments that felt like hours. Finally, I felt a small kick. I could begin to breathe again. We were both okay.

I was taken to the hospital to be evaluated and kept overnight. They put me on a fetal monitor to watch for contractions and to monitor his little heartbeat. Hearing that heartbeat all night long was the most beautiful sound I had ever heard. The next day, I had the MRI, which would look at Jude's brain. I remember being in the machine, praying, and running through every worship song I could think of. So much had happened. I wanted to believe that he was healthy and that everything had changed after that life-changing prayer, but until I held him in my arms, I couldn't fully accept that he was okay.

One week later, our doctor called with the MRI results. He said that it didn't show anything different from the ultrasound and that he truly believed everything was going to be just fine. This was a huge answer to prayer. God continued to show up for us in all of this. I couldn't believe how faithful God had been through this entire process.

There were times during this pregnancy when I was crippled by fear and anxiety and when I worried that I wasn't strong enough to keep going. I feared that I would not be equipped to care for a child with special needs or to be the mother that my son deserved. At one point, I was scared that I would fail graduate school. I had lost my focus. I had become consumed with my pregnancy and my life outside of school. I worried about the complications that might occur during delivery and if God would continue to carry us through.

In those hard, treacherous moments, I did something that I had not done in my past. I got on my knees—actually on my face—in prayer and submission. I knew that every part of this process was completely out of my control but was also permitted by my Heavenly Father. God had been pursuing me all of my life, and finally in this process, he made me fall recklessly in love with him and all that he is.

You may have experienced a time like this. Maybe your back was against a wall, and you could not see what God was doing or what his purpose was in the unknown. If you haven't experienced anything like this, at some point, you will. It's in those moments that God is closer than ever. It's in the pain and the unknown that he is there waiting for us to sprint to him. He always accepts us and loves us fully and completely, despite our doubts and messes.

My son was born on New Year's Eve, just over six years ago.

His birthday could not be more fitting as everything about him represented something new. He was the miracle that God knew I needed. He is meant to be here. I have no doubt that God has a purpose for him. He was the child that God used to draw me to himself and forever change the path of my life.

My son was born perfectly healthy. He does not have an ounce of developmental delay or any genetic disorders. He is special with a capital S. Somehow even at his young age, everyone he interacts with picks up on this. We have faced challenges with his health, but they have been completely unrelated to what was noted during my pregnancy. He has asthma and an IgG deficiency (immune system issue), which has come with its own set of challenges, but none of that could have been predicted.

Pay attention to the words *none of that could have been predicted*. We don't dictate everything that happens in our lives, but God does. We will inevitably face unforeseen challenges over and over again, but God gives us the tools to navigate life and to find complete freedom.

I'm reminded every day that my son is an example of God's goodness. God honored me when he didn't have to. I don't know why he chose to allow our son to be born without any of the challenges that the first perinatologist was sure existed. I don't know if those variations existed, but our son was healed and the course of his life was changed when we were prayed over. I believe that's possible because I knew at that moment that everything had changed.

This was the biggest black-balloon pop of my life. Since then, I have been a different person. God finally got through to me. He used the small mustard seed of faith that I had held onto all of my life and grew it exponentially. It took something like this to provoke total surrender. Now that I have it and know what this feels like, I'm never going back.

## It's Your Turn

Do you have a story about surrendering?

_____

_____

_____

_____

Reflect on your life for a moment and then list a scenario in which God showed up for you in a big way.

_____

_____

_____

_____

If you have not experienced a surrender black balloon yet, what are some ways you can lean into the Lord in preparation for the unexpected?

_____

_____

_____

_____

## Words to Help You Pop the Black Balloon

Trust in the Lord with all your heart and lean not on your own understanding. (Proverbs 3:5)

Blessed is the one who perseveres under trial because, having stood the test, that person will receive the crown of life that the Lord has promised to those who love him. (James 1:12)

I keep my eyes always on the Lord. With him at my right hand, I will not be shaken. Therefore my heart is glad and my tongue rejoices; my body also will rest secure. (Psalm 16 :8–9)

I prayed for this child, and the Lord has granted me what I asked of him. (1 Samuel 1:27)

# Chapter 9

# The Layoff Black Balloon

After you pop many of the black balloons in your life and surrender your life to Christ, life becomes super easy. I'm just kidding. This is an erroneous statement. If you believe this, bless your little heart. You are in for a rude awakening. It doesn't get easier, but it gets crazier, more complicated, and more challenging. I know that you must be screaming, "Sign me up! I can't wait to surrender my life to Christ!"

Hear me out. This black balloon came after my surrender and taught us more than we could have imagined. Yet again, God showed up in my life in a very unexpected way and taught my husband and me some lessons that we will surely hold on to forever.

No matter where we are in our career paths, having job security is something that we all want. We want to know that we will be able to provide for our families and ourselves. We want to grow in our careers and feel financially stable. We put the work in and hope that it will be recognized and rewarded in one way or another. If you're doing the hardest job of all—you're at home raising babies—I know that you are hoping that your partner will be able to provide a stable income for the family.

Stability is a beautiful thing. It is awesome, until it's not, and you don't have it anymore. The funny thing is that we don't realize how much we appreciate our mundane lives until they are anything but mundane. This goes for anything, including our health, our jobs, or being able to see the people we love when we want to see them. Our mundane lives can change in an instant.

One Saturday afternoon, my husband, my kids, and I went to a friend's house. We were all hanging out and having a great time. We began to talk about our jobs and our current situations.

My husband and some of our friends were in pharmaceutical sales. It's a great profession, and they receive a lot of perks. I'm not going to lie. There have been numerous times that I have questioned the reason I chose nursing and didn't choose their route. I enjoy hearing them talk because it's so different from my career's world. It's interesting in a completely different way. Our discussions aren't focused on someone's life, an interesting case, or an extremely stressful day at the hospital or in the clinic. I love these types of conversations that I have with my medical friends and peers, but now and then, it's fun to talk about something else.

Anyway, we were chatting about things, and I distinctly remember my husband saying, "I hope I get laid off when the next round comes. That way, I can keep the severance. This new opportunity is coming through, and I'm about to put in my notice anyway."

I almost died. I stopped in my tracks and thought, *Take it back! Take it back! Lord, he did not say that. He didn't mean it. Please don't use this to teach us something.*

Insert God looking down on us shaking his head and saying, "Oh I will teach you, my children, just you wait."

This conversation happened on a Saturday at the end of November. My husband was laid off the following week and at the start of December. He was laid off before the most expensive month of the year. Have I mentioned that both of our children were also born in December? Did I also mention that each year in December, we plan a family trip and give it to each other as a gift instead of something material? Our beautiful winter-wonderland family vacation to Chicago had already been planned. We had announced it to our little cherubs. My husband also carried our health insurance. Yep, all of these things were happening, and my husband was jobless at Christmastime. It had all happened essentially after he had asked for it because he was so sure about the new opportunity, which he had been interviewing for.

Even though we didn't want this to be our reality, it was. At the end of the first week of him not having a job, his company car was picked up from our driveway. Our family's insurance would be ending within the next three weeks. I found myself taking an Uber ride to work so that my husband could have our car to take our kids to and from daycare.

Let me tell you about these morning Uber rides at 6:00 a.m. and some mornings, at 7 a.m. The caliber of people driving for Uber at that time is unlike anything I have ever seen. One morning, I was sure that either my driver was drunk or whoever had been in the car with him before me had been because it reeked of alcohol. I also think that he may have been living in his car. It was interesting, to say the least.

I made it to work safely that morning and had him drive me to the back of the building so that none of my coworkers or even worse, my patients would see me getting out of a dirty car with a random man who smelled like a brewery. Ah, yes, they are such beautiful memories.

We decided that since most of our family vacation was already paid for, we should still go. We also wanted to keep things as normal as possible for our kids. We knew that some level of severance would be coming, which was a huge blessing, but we didn't know how much. We were also relying on the fact that this other job opportunity, which my husband had been interviewing for, was going to be a sure thing. I had been praying heavily, and I knew God had us in this place for a reason. It was not fun by any stretch of the imagination, but I trusted that he would come through for us, that this other job opportunity would work out, and that everything would be hunky-dory again.

We were sitting at the airport on our way to Chicago when my husband got a call from the new company. We were under the impression that it was going to be a discussion about his start date. How perfect this was, right? He would get his start date just before we were on our way to a vacation, and we would have nothing to worry about. The vacation would be amazing, and we would be celebrating his new job. Oh, bless us. We were so wrong.

They were calling to let him know that they were still planning to hire him but that his start date was going to be exponentially extended—so extended that they couldn't give us a time frame. They were still interested in him and assured him that he was their guy. I saw the shock and dismay on his face as he ended the call. I could sense a bit of panic for the first time since the layoff. We went ahead and boarded the plane as if nothing had happened. We wanted to enjoy this time as a family and make all the special memories we could with our kids, even during this turmoil.

I remember being on the plane and praying. I was asking God for guidance, provision, and peace. I knew that no matter what, he was at work here. It was just a lot to process.

When we got back, we had to figure out what our next step was going to be. Thank God that I was able to put our family on my job's insurance plan, but we still had to figure out what to do about my husband's career. He couldn't exactly sit around jobless waiting for this other opportunity to come through when we had no time frame to go on. He started to explore other options, and we even considered moving to another state for an opportunity.

I definitely had moments of fear, but because I had experienced surrender and I now knew that God was for me and not against me, I trusted him. Once you surrender in that way, you handle big things differently. I had some rough days, but I knew that God was allowing this for a reason. I had seen his goodness, and I knew that it was real.

Weeks went by, and my husband still didn't have a job. He was even turned down from another great company after he had gotten to the final interview. God was not playing around at this point.

Life got messier. Our son got sick on Christmas Day with some sort of stomach flu. It was very bad, and we all ended up getting it. New Year's Eve came, and as I mentioned, it was my son's birthday. He was doing much better, and we had all shaken the plague at that point. But that afternoon, I got a call from my dad. He sounded awful. I had never heard him sound like this. He was short of breath.

I put everything on hold and headed to his house. When I got there, I found my dad in terrible pain. His stomach was hurting, and he also said that he felt like he was going to pass out. My dad is not a small man, so I knew that if he passed out or fell, I wasn't going to be able to get him up. My poor stepmom had caught the plague from us too so she was in no position to help.

I had brought my stethoscope with me, so I went ahead and listened to my dad's heart. He was dizzy for a reason. I could tell right away that he was in atrial fibrillation (had an irregular heart rhythm), which was completely new for him. I called 911. There was no way I could get him into the car by myself and take him to the hospital in the state that he was in. I followed the ambulance to the hospital. My stepmom should not be around other humans, so I had her stay home to rest.

After all of our stuff, my dad and I were facing some real-life issues. It felt surreal. I tried to put together the events of the last few weeks. I had ended up in the hospital with my dad, and I was concerned that he could have something very serious going on. It was a lot.

Did you know that when you are faced with extreme stress, your marriage thrives? Again, I'm kidding. We were doing anything but thriving at that time. We weren't even going to be together on our son's birthday or for New Year's. While I was at the hospital with my dad, my husband and I got in a stupid argument about something. I honestly can't remember what it was about, but we attacked each other. I was trying to set it all aside and be there for my dad, but it all felt like too much. That New Year's Eve, it felt like my world was crashing. The hope and peace that I had been experiencing were fading. I kept praying, but God started to feel distant.

My dad's heart rate stabilized but remained in atrial fibrillation. He looked at me and told me to hurry home so that I could bring in the New Year with my husband. I was grateful to him for this and respected that even in his state, he was looking out for me. I kissed him goodbye and headed home, fully expecting my husband to be up waiting for me. We would make up, put the events of the day and last few weeks behind us, and bring in the new year with a whole new perspective.

Nope, I was sorely mistaken. My husband was already in bed asleep, as were the kids. I was alone in my living room with Ryan Seacrest and a pool of my tears. I wanted to believe it would all be okay. I wanted to feel relief and trust God's timing, but it was all very hard.

Now that I was different, I did things differently. Instead of staying angry, I opted to do my best to show grace. Instead of blaming God, I leaned into him. I spent time journaling, prayed, and read books and devotions. I started serving at church even though it seemed like terrible timing to start. Take note of that. When you think that your life is in a low place, go serve someone else. You will quickly realize that you are not in that low of a place. God will work on you in a way that you need it and even though you don't think you do.

Things started to change. God came in and started to do the work. My heart and my husband's heart began to soften. We worked together as a team to figure everything out. The more we committed everything to the Lord, the more we were at peace and saw him moving.

## The Balloon Pops

On New Year's Day, my husband and I had a very civilized conversation. Things began to take a turn for the better. We talked about the hard stuff and everything that we both had been harboring inside during the storm we had been facing over that last month. I felt like everything at home was in a good enough place that I could go back to the hospital and see my dad.

When I got there, I could immediately see that he was feeling better. His heart still wasn't in normal rhythm, but he was so much more at ease, and we were able to have a real conversation. God did this. He put both of us in that hospital room on that day to share the moment that we did. We had a deep conversation, and healing continued to take place. I saw a man whom I truly loved lying in that bed instead of a man whom I resented. His love for the Lord flowed from him, and I felt how real it was with every fiber of my being. Our relationship had changed, and I know we were both so grateful for that.

Healing like that cannot be explained. Only God can do something like this.

My dad and I remain close. We share an extremely special bond. I know how loved he is by our Heavenly Father. Yes, there was a time in my life when he was not the earthly father that I so badly needed. But because of our Heavenly Father and all that he is, we have both been set free from our pasts and have the relationship that we do today. We're proof that it's never too late and that God can rectify something that seems so unlikely.

I felt blessed to be there for him and thankful that he wanted me there. We were both experiencing the extreme freedom that God can give in those moments together.

Once I was back home, my husband and I decided that it was a new year and that we needed to hit the reset button. We put in the work. My husband ended up taking a less-than-ideal job to provide for our family. God blessed us with a second car so that my husband could do the driving he needed to do for his new job. I continued to serve in our church and even found other ways to help people.

I've said this in previous chapters, but it's so important that I need to say it again: God is never closer to someone than when he is close to the brokenhearted and those who are struggling. He was leaning into us, and we continued to lean into him. I suppose that because of this, he chose to bless us. He will do the same thing for you if you let him. We fight it. Letting him win is the black balloon pop that he is looking for.

That first month of the new year, I went from using an Uber car to get to work with my aforementioned friend, who was living in his alcohol-ridden car, to driving a beautiful new vehicle that God had provided for us. My husband went from working a less-than-ideal job that was paying the bills to getting hired by the company he had previously been interviewing with. God provided for us financially in unexpected and unseen ways in the months to come.

Our marriage got stronger, and we were in awe of what God had done for us. My relationship with my dad was completely rectified, and we were walking with immense purpose in our relationships with Christ. The layoff black balloon brought so much healing in many ways. Without it, we would not be where we are today.

God taught us that what comes out of our mouths during this process is extremely vital. He's listening, but the enemy is also listening. Our words can be used for us, but they can also be used against us. My husband and I watched this play out in a huge way. Again, God did not have to honor us, but he chose to.

If you are in a place of transition or waiting and you or someone you love is facing a layoff or job transition, trust me when I say that I know how incredibly difficult this is. I know that it stirs up emotions. It brings out the worst in relationships. This black balloon is tough—they all are, but this one causes us to question many things and challenges us in ways we couldn't have expected. Do your best to arm yourself with God's grace. Seek him every opportunity that you can. Do anything and everything possible to keep yourself positive. Serve others even if it seems ridiculous to do so. If your partner is facing a job loss or transition, give them grace. Even when it is far from fathomable, give them grace. Pray a lot and be very specific in your requests.

I write my requests down so that when they are answered, I can look back and visibly see what I was asking God for. When I go back and read my prayer journal, I can feel the emotion in the pages. I can distinctly remember how I felt in those moments and can sense the desperation in my requests.

God is listening and walking with us through all of these desperate moments. His Word is there for us to dive into and to seek answers from. He shows up for people repeatedly in the Bible. He is the same God to us that he was to Job, Abraham, and Moses. If you're in waiting, your time is coming. Lean in to God. Allow God to equip and use you in ways that only he can. He will provide all you need and more.

## It's Your Turn

Have you ever experienced a layoff or job loss black balloon?

_____

_____

_____

_____

What did you learn from this experience and in what ways did God show up for you?

_____

_____

_____

_____

Has something you have said ever been used against you?

_____

_____

_____

_____

How can you equip yourself to handle an unexpected career situation?

_____

_____

_____

_____

## Words to Help You Pop the Black Balloon

So is my word that goes out from my mouth: It will not return to me empty, but will accomplish what I desire and achieve the purpose for which I sent it. (Isaiah 55:11)

The tongue has the power of life and death, and those who love it will eat its fruit.(Proverbs 18:21)

May the God of hope fill you with all joy and peace as you trust in him, so that you may overflow with hope by the power of the Holy Spirit. (Romans 15:13)

# Chapter 10

# Keeping the Black Balloons Deflated

If you aren't facing any black balloons in your life right now, there's a good chance you'll be handed one at some point. Maybe you have been handed one in the past. Taking the steps to pop the black balloons in our lives is not an easy task. It takes work, reflection, and commitment. For me, it has also taken a ton of faith and focusing on finding out who God truly is. When I reflect on how he has shown up for me over and over again and in all of my pain and fear, his pattern of goodness is revealed.

After writing this and putting all of the work into it, I stand here to tell you that he is who he says he is. God never promised that we wouldn't face challenges, devastation, consequences, or hardships in our lives. However, he is the one thing that never changes in any of these circumstances. He may seem distant and almost nonexistent at times. You may deeply question your faith or the reason something so terrible is happening in your or your loved one's life. I still have these questions. I don't think that we are meant to have all of the answers, but what I do know is that God is walking with us every step of the way.

The things in my life that used to define me and bring fear, anxiety, depression, and deep-seated pain no longer hold any power over me. God gave me every tool that I need to pop these black balloons and experience full freedom in him. He has used unlikely people to speak to me, created key opportunities for my deliverance, and brought me freedom from situations in my life that seemed completely hopeless, even when I had my back turned on him.

I hope that after reading these chapters, you can reflect on your own life and see God's hand in it. I also want you to know and to remember that he is not done with you. Every part of you was designed perfectly by our Heavenly Father, and because of that, he uses your uniqueness to prosper you.

I know, too well, how hard it is to surrender. I'm sure that some of your black balloons are far worse and more tragic than the ones I have faced. The pain that exists in this world runs deeper than I care to imagine. It seems impossible that we can be redeemed and can walk blamelessly and fully with a good God, who has already taken on the weight of all of our sin and pain for us. But it's true. God sent his only son to die for us and to set us free.

Are there days when this is hard to believe? Yes, of course. But when you think God is done with you and your situation, I encourage you to channel that small mustard seed of faith so that you might have and see what he can do with it.

If you're still carrying the weight of one or many black balloons in your life, I encourage you to acknowledge this and to begin popping them. God can take your greatest pain and failures and use them to bring more good than you can fathom. If you're not in a place to embrace total surrender, take some baby steps toward the pop. Here are a few:

- Research counselors.
- Decide to sit in church and actually take notes on the message.
- Find a short daily devotion that incorporates scripture.
- Check out a new and uplifting podcast.
- Open up to a friend or a family member about your problems.
- Meditate.
- Go for walk or try a small workout regimen on a daily basis.

- Do something you truly enjoy regularly.
- Change your diet for the better.
- Commit to getting the sleep your body needs.
- Set a small obtainable goal and map out what it would take for you to achieve it.

You are definitely destined for more. You are meant to live in freedom. You are loved more than you could imagine by a Heavenly Father who is so good.

I can't promise that there won't be more black balloons. In fact, they are still handed to me all over the place. The difference is that I now handle them more healthily and productively. Well, I don't always do that. Sometimes my old behaviors and negative mindset start to set in, but as soon as I notice it happening, I take the appropriate steps to rectify it and to get back on track. This takes daily work and commitment, but it's worth it.

My identity is no longer defined by my past, social status, marriage, family, social-media following, job, or accomplishments. My identity is defined by who God says I am, and so is yours. God says that we are loved, forgiven, and free. This is who I really am.

Your black balloons are not placed there to destroy you. It may seem that way, but each of these obstacles has caused you to grow and has helped you to overcome and grow a little closer to the person God sees you as—the person who has endless potential and can go further than anyone would think. Your story is unique, delicate, and believe it or not, a perfectly written melody by our Heavenly Father.

He knows what decisions we will make before we make them. He knows the hard things that are coming. He also knows the triumph that we will get to in the end. We are already victorious. Let that sink in. We are already victorious! We're covered and loved beyond measure, regardless of what we've done, what we've experienced, or whom we've been told we are.

I still stand by the fact that I'm not anyone special in the sea of incredibly talented and amazing humans in this world. I'm a hot mess, which God has pursued heavily and recklessly. I'm here to tell all of you about it. Nothing in my life has happened by chance. Nothing in yours has either.

We have a choice when it comes to how we handle what we're dealt. For many years, I tried to handle it on my own. I grabbed my black balloons and desperately tried to pop them. You've seen the little two-year-old who tries to sit on a balloon to pop it, but it keeps slipping out from under that child's little tushy. Yeah, that is me as I try to pop my major life black balloons on my own but to no avail. Eventually, a parent comes along to help the two-year-old pop the balloon, and then a huge smile of accomplishment graces that child's face.

I serve the God who comes in, pulls me off my tushy, and helps me pop my black balloons and find pure joy and freedom. There is so much good to be experienced. I still feel like I've only seen the bare minimum. I know God has so much more for me and for you. I hope that you will embrace this and do whatever it takes to finally pop the black balloons in your life. There's freedom waiting for you. Now go out and get it.

## Words to Help You Pop the Black Balloon

Do not conform to the pattern of this world, but be transformed by the renewing of your mind. Then you will be able to test and approve what God's will is—his good, pleasing and perfect will. (Romans 12:2)

Trust in the Lord with all your heart and lean not on your own understanding; in all your ways submit to him, and he will make your paths straight. (Proverbs 3: 5–6)

The thief comes only to steal and kill and destroy;
I have come that they may have life, and have it to
the full. (John 10:10)

What good is it for someone to gain the whole world,
yet forfeit their soul? (Mark 8:36)

CPSIA information can be obtained
at www.ICGtesting.com
Printed in the USA
LVHW092357120120
643403LV00001B/259/P